Corbyn

Corbyn

The Strange Rebirth
of Radical Politics

Richard Seymour

VERSO
London • New York

First published by Verso 2016
© Richard Seymour 2016

The moral rights of the author have been asserted

1 3 5 7 9 10 8 6 4 2

Verso
UK: 6 Meard Street, London W1F 0EG
US: 20 Jay Street, Suite 1010, Brooklyn, NY 11201
versobooks.com

Verso is the imprint of New Left Books

ISBN-13: 978-1-78478-531-4
ISBN-13: 978-1-78478-532-1 (UK EBK)
ISBN-13: 978-1-78478-533-8 (US EBK)

British Library Cataloguing in Publication Data
A catalogue record for this book is available from the British Library

Library of Congress Cataloging-in-Publication Data

Names: Seymour, Richard, 1977– author.
Title: Corbyn : the crisis of British politics / Richard Seymour.
Description: London ; Brooklyn, NY : Verso, 2016.
Identifiers: LCCN 2016019162 | ISBN 9781784785314 (paperback) | ISBN
  9781784785321 (ebook : U.K.) | ISBN 9781784785338 (ebook : U.S.)
Subjects: LCSH: Corbyn, Jeremy. | Labour Party (Great Britain) – Biography. |
  Politicians – Great Britain – Biography. | Legislators – Great
  Britain – Biography. | Great Britain. Parliament. House of
  Commons – Biography. | Labour Party (Great Britain) – History. |
  Radicalism – Great Britain – History. | Democracy – Great Britain – History. |
  Great Britain – Politics and government – 1997–2007. | Great
  Britain – Politics and government – 2007– | BISAC: POLITICAL SCIENCE /
  Political Process / General. | HISTORY / Europe / Great Britain.
Classification: LCC JN1129.L32 S443 2016 | DDC 328.41092 [B] – dc23
LC record available at https://lccn.loc.gov/2016019162

Typeset in Fournier by MJ & N Gavan, Truro, Cornwall
Printed in the UK by CPI Group (UK) Ltd, Croydon, CR0 4YY

Contents

Acknowledgements

This book was proposed, researched and written in a flush of enthusiasm after Jeremy Corbyn won the leadership of the Labour Party – a most unexpected occasion for a book. It couldn't have been completed to my satisfaction without the input and encouragement of several friends, colleagues and many Labour members.

Marsha-Jane Thompson, Ben Sellers, Liam Young, Margaret Corvid, Phil Burton-Cartledge and Simon Hewitt were among those who gave up their free time and thoughts, and I gained a lot from their experience and knowledge. Robin Archer at the London School of Economics offered me the benefit of his considerable expertise and thoughtful analyses. Jeremy Gilbert of Compass was also, as always, incredibly insightful.

In addition, there were many individuals, Labour activists, and others who, though too modest to be named, were happy to help fill in the blanks, and explained Labour politics in a way that the mainstream press generally can't. They did this despite knowing that they may not agree with my analysis. Huge thanks to them.

My editor, Rosie Warren, has been amazingly efficient, tolerant and helpful throughout, and I'm immensely appreciative of everything she has done.

Finally, thanks to my agent, Susie Nicklin, for her advice, support, insight and hard work in helping this book to come about.

Introduction:
Against All Odds

There's Something about Jeremy

Early 2016, and Tony Blair is 'baffled'. What with Jeremy Corbyn in Britain, and Bernie Sanders in the United States, he sighs: 'I'm not sure I fully understand politics right now.'[1]

His confusion is to be expected. He had warned Labour, to no avail: 'if your heart is with Jeremy, get a transplant'. His former confederate Peter Mandelson joined in, telling that bastion of Labour values the *Financial Times* that: 'The Labour Party is in mortal danger.' And his old ally and sparring partner Gordon Brown exhorted Labour not to become a 'party of permanent protest'.[2] What more could they have done?

But since Blair left office, the world has been changing, one regime at a time, and he is no longer at ease. Sarkozy has gone, Bush has gone, Aznar has gone, Mubarak has gone, Qadhafi has gone. Soon, his last ally in office will be the Kazakhstani dictator, Nursultan Nazarbayev, for whom he provided invaluable service in managing his image after a notorious regime massacre.[3]

As abroad, so it is at home. Where once the Blairites seemed unshakeable in their power, their ruthless sodality has finally bitten the dust in Labour's leadership elections of 2015, when they received 4.5 per cent of the vote. Officially, the burial was executed by an unassuming anti-war socialist named Jeremy Corbyn, who won with a landslide 59.5 per cent of the vote in the first round.

It would be underselling this to call it the most unlikely political comeback in history. It is true that there was a time when socialists operated openly in the Labour Party, unashamed and relatively vocal. Yet rumours of their former power have always been exaggerated. And this is the first time in Labour's history that it has a radical social-ist for a leader.

It does the novelty of the situation no justice at all to compare Corbyn to Michael Foot, as some commenta-tors prematurely did. Foot was of the soft-Left, and his political roots belonged in a form of radicalised liberalism. Despite a certain amnesia on this point, moreover, he was far more dependent upon the party's right-wing than its hard-Left – it was the former which ran the ill-fated 1983 election campaign. His long record of peace campaigning didn't prevent him from supporting Mrs Thatcher in the Falklands, in a way that it is difficult to conceive of Corbyn doing. A closer historical comparison might possibly be made with George Lansbury, a left-wing pacifist with an activist past, who was elected Labour leader in 1931 after Ramsay MacDonald's defection to join a Conservative-led National Government. That one has to look back this far for comparison is a register of precisely how unprecedented the current position of the Labour Party is, and even here it only goes so far: Lansbury had been a popular local mayor and a cabinet member by the time he was elected, whereas Corbyn has held no executive office. That this rebounded to his advantage in this campaign tells something of how unpopular the governing strata has become.

Jeremy Corbyn is one of the last standing Bennites in the Labour Party. Those whose memory of Tony Benn is chiefly of a gentle elder radical in the anti-war movement and incomparable diarist, rather than as a threat to the British establishment hounded by spooks and monstered on the front pages, may not immediately grasp the significance of this. For Benn had been an upper-class rebel, a noble by birth who rejected his title, and a former cabinet minister who had seen inside the vaults of power and concluded that it called for something rather more wide-reaching than mere tinkering. He could, by all accounts, have led Labour himself had he not veered so hard to the left having experienced office. But the experience of 'office without power', as he described it, radicalised him.[4] Labour's problem, he argued, had been that it attempted to manage capitalism rather than do anything to undermine the serious inequities of wealth and power that existed at the time. As a result, it was presiding over a system that was losing legitimacy, generating major discontent, and as a result was in danger of being reversed by the Right.

To remedy this perceived failure, Benn had called for Labour to implement a round of sweeping reforms, akin in its depth and ambition to the achievements of the 1945 Labour Government. This meant redistributing wealth, reforming unelected state apparatuses, and nationalising key industries in order to place them under workers' control. One of his major criticisms of the post-war settlement had been that nationalised industries were still not democratic, but run on the same top-down basis as private industry – often by the same people. Within the framework of democratic socialism, he argued, it should be possible for parliament to pass laws giving workers the right to manage and to elect their managers.[5] The very idea that Labour should ever aspire to such drastic reforms was precisely what New Labour existed to destroy.

Corbyn, from a more humble background in rural Shropshire, where he worked on local farms, has never been considered a likely Labour leader. As he put it,

> The difference between Tony and me was that whereas he was one of those very unusual politicians who was actually very successful in a conventional career pattern, I have been monumentally unsuccessful in the conventional career pattern.[6]

Yet in another way, his political background was more favourable to a course as a socialist agitator than Benn's. The son of middle-class political activists who met while campaigning for the republican side in the Spanish Civil War, he grew up in a family steeped in radical ideas. And the evidence is that he genuinely obsessed about politics and little else. As a grammar school student, he foreswore study the better to spend time with his politics. As a Voluntary Service Overseas worker in Jamaica, he was radicalised by the 'imperialist attitudes, social division, and economic exploitation' he found there. As a trade union organiser, first in the National Union of Tailors and Garment Workers, and then in the National Union of Public Employees, he tirelessly attended meetings, protests and picket lines. He seems to have found no time at all either for money or drink or for the hedonistic pleasures of counterculture, preferring instead to practise the teetotal strain of socialism for which Benn was famous. On the plus side, this meant that he was, as his former partner Jane Chapman recalled, 'very principled, very honest ... a genuinely nice guy'.[7]

These characteristics are consistently evident throughout Corbyn's career as constituency MP for Islington North, which he has represented since 1983. Even his most sceptical biographer, the *Telegraph* journalist Rosa Prince, acknowledges that he 'is known as a "good constituency MP", meaning he takes great pains over helping those who need him, and he is universally considered to do an exemplary job'.[8] As a member of the Socialist Campaign Group, representing the Bennite wing of Labour, he has consistently opposed the government whichever party was in office. Ever the activist, never an operator, he was more likely to be found working for the Anti-Apartheid Movement or the Palestine Solidarity Campaign than wheeling and dealing for favour and influence. He was found, during the expenses scandal that befell British parliamentarians in 2009, to have claimed the smallest sum of expenses of any MP – £8.95 for a printer cartridge.[9]

His activism is not just a moral calling, but also a matter of a conscious political strategy. 'People are saying the job of the PLP is to go for the middle-class suburban vote,' he explained during the Kinnock era,

> but the Campaign Group must be on the picket lines and at the workplace level. In inner-city areas where there are no major employers except local government and some public services, there just isn't trade union experience, and school-leavers know nothing about the trade union or labour movement.[10]

For Corbyn, the relative weakening of the Left and the labour movement was not a reason to move to the right, but to patiently rebuild. This is far more fundamental to his perspective for reviving the Labour Party than the necessary compromises and reassurances offered to parliamentary backbenchers. As he explained in one of his campaign speeches, the Conservatives were able to win because people were not mobilised and thus didn't vote:

> Their parliamentary majority is based on a low turnout, it's based on the support of 24% of the electorate as a whole … There is a fairly small political party membership in Britain, really. The Labour Party membership is 240,000. I've no idea what the Conservative Party membership figure is … Liberal Democrat membership I have no idea; I suspect it's not very big. And so there isn't a vast number of people in political parties in Britain, but that's not to say we're living in a totally depoliticised society. Look at the 250,000

that came on the anti-austerity march last weekend; look at the vast number of people who were on the Pride march in London yesterday, and the demonstration. People are involved in politics in a different way ... I think we need to build a social movement.[11]

This is not to claim that Corbyn's campaign *was* the social movement, but it used the techniques of movement building in a way that conveyed what Corbyn wanted for the Labour Party. This way of doing politics, greatly underestimated by the media and political classes, was critical to Corbyn's success. The exhausting sequence of packed public meetings in towns and cities across the country, for example, were a typical part of Corbyn's calendar. As he explained, 'I did over a hundred events during the leadership campaign and by the end of the year I will probably have done 400 to 500 public meetings.'[12] This political style had been largely forgotten in the era of focus groups, marketised politics and the obsessive shaping of news cycles. Corbyn, far from evincing embarrassment at his militant record, plentiful images of which circulated on social media sites during his campaign, embraced it as a virtue. He was elected as a man of the movements, not of the markets.

And through such means, he has assembled a surprising breadth of support. The ideas that he champions haven't had a powerful mainstream voice for years, and the last time anyone remotely this left-wing got close to the Labour leadership was during Tony Benn's run for deputy leader in 1981, which Corbyn played a leading role in organising. As Phil Burton-Cartledge, a Labour Party member in Stoke, astutely observed, Corbyn seems to have personified something that people of various political hues feel is missing from politics. 'Whether you're a Green, self-described Old Labour, a recovering Trotskyist, or some other permutation', there is 'something attractive about Jeremy's politics'.[13]

This is what has taken the party establishment and its sympathisers in the media most by surprise. The ideas with which Corbyn won are ones that have largely been ignored, suppressed, or regarded with amused condescension since the Blairites took control. It was not just that Corbyn was prepared to oppose the government's austerity programmes and support higher public spending, nationalisation and redistribution. This was all bread and butter for the social-democratic Left. And on these issues, there is some evidence that the British electorate is more left-wing than is conventionally assumed.[14] Corbyn also defied what is supposed to be the common sense view on immigration, refusing to give an inch to the resentful UKIP-style nationalism that had permeated both of the dominant parties. This suggests that Corbyn is prepared to challenge more than the establishment; he aims to run against popular prejudice, and win. His first gesture as leader, utterly characteristic of him, was to attend a pro-refugees rally in central London, where he received what the *Mirror* called a 'hero's welcome'.[15]

The agenda on which Corbyn was elected is not, however, the stuff of which revolutions are made. He has pledged to end austerity, and in its stead implement a People's Quantitative Easing programme with money invested in infrastructural development, job-creation and high-technology industries. Canadian Prime Minister Justin

Trudeau won office on an agenda like this. Even the OECD is anti-austerity these days.[16] He promises to address the housing crisis through extensive home-building, to fully nationalise the railways, and to bring all academies back under local democratic control. These objectives are to be funded, not so much by squeezing the rich like a sponge to water the gardens of the poor, as by closing tax loopholes, stimulating growth, and spending less on controversial programmes such as Trident.

This is in most ways a classic social-democratic remedy, which could easily have come with some Wilsonian vocables about 'the white heat of technological revolution'. The problem for the establishment is not necessarily Corbyn's agenda. It may be too radical for today's Labour Party, today's media and today's parliamentary spectrum, but business could live with it, and the consensus would shift if Corbyn gained popular support. The problem is the type of politician that he is. The political tendency represented by Corbyn was supposed to be finished, the very idea of an alternative to capitalism interred since 1989 and all that. Now, it is not terribly shocking to read of surveys that show British people to be slightly 'keener on socialism than on capitalism'.[17] It is not the case that the Left is suddenly vibrant and full of beans and power. It is the case that, in circumstances which defy analogy, there is a chance for radical politics to make an utterly unexpected rebirth.

How did he do it? In this book, I argue that Corbyn intelligently exploited an opening which has come about from the decay of the old parties. This isn't just Labour's problem, despite the obvious complacency and enervation of the party's traditional elites. As of writing, the Tories are undergoing the latest spasm of a chronic crisis pivoted on Europe, but affecting a far wider range of issues. Corbyn, despite the weakness of his position and the extraordinary belligerence of his back benchers, has succeeded in exploiting these divisions to force policy retreats on a series of issues, from tax credits, to the Saudi prisons contract, to disability benefits cuts. But his own party is in no better shape. The logic working itself out in all the major parliamentary parties tends toward splits and realignment. This malaise goes deeper than policy and leadership.

The story of Corbyn's victory is one in which parliamentary democracy, and the traditionally dominant parties, have been slowly sliding into a crisis of legitimacy for some time – and that crisis suddenly became acute with the onset of economic stagnation and austerity. The representative link, between the people and the government, has been breaking down for decades. Now it is throwing up new forms of political volatility. The SNP's surge in Scotland, and UKIP's surge in England, are recent manifestations of this breakdown and realignment of political loyalties. If Corbyn's surge was far more rapid and less anticipated, he and his team were just the latest group of radical Leftists to punch well above their weight because they saw where the establishment was failing and articulated the right ideas. Whether it is Syriza in Greece, or Podemos in Spain, or even Sanders in the United States, the sudden surges in support for individuals and groups who were previously marginalised arises from the same type of crisis.

These examples, of course, also contain certain warnings to Corbyn and his supporters. Podemos, despite having led in the polls, was ultimately unable to secure an election victory. Syriza, having won, was unable to change policy despite forming a government. Sanders may yet win, but is already warning his supporters that even as president the scale of resistance he would face from 'the billionaire class' could make it all but impossible for him to implement his goals. Corbyn, of course, is some way from being in a position to tangle with 'the billionaire class'. He has first to face down the bile of his own parliamentary colleagues such as David Blunkett, Tristram Hunt, Simon Danczuk, Sadiq Khan, Caroline Flint, John Mann, Michael Dugher and Ben Bradshaw. He also has to keep a shadow cabinet together against a steady drumbeat of more subtly undermining behaviour on the part of Hillary Benn, Maria Eagle and deputy leader Tom Watson. And he has to weather the attacks from the Conservatives and the media, whose criticisms invariably seem to resonate with those of Corbyn's Labour critics.

In the coming chapters, I will explain how Corbyn faced down 'Project Fear' and won, before delving into the broader context and history of British politics and Labour's role in it. In asking whether Corbyn has any chance of success as a Labour leader, let alone as a prime minister, the answers I give won't leave anyone entirely comfortable. Those awaiting a return to 'politics as usual' will find a lot to be worried about. The Blairites and Labour's 'moderates' will find the analysis hugely disagreeable. Corbynistas, meanwhile, won't find a tone of cheerleading optimism here. Above all, although this book is written in sympathy with Corbyn, it is not written with any loyalty to the Labour Party, of which I am not a member. That fact allows me to put my finger on what might be the raw nerve of any Labour loyalist, left or right: that the party may simply be untenable in its current form. Because the most difficult challenges that Corbyn faces have to do with the question he was elected to answer: whither Labour? Labour's decline is what Corbyn was elected to address. Labour's decline is what gave him the space to lead. And Labour's decline will now constitute the major obstacle to his success.

1
How 'Project Fear' Failed

Let us remind ourselves of the extraordinary facts of this leadership election. When the race began, Corbyn was considered a no-hope candidate. As an anti-austerity, anti-war campaigner, he was far too remote from the conventional idea of a successful politician to win. *Channel 4* journalist Michael Crick summed up this logic when he wrote to his Twitter followers: 'Under my law of leadership elections – that the freshest and/or youngest contender usually wins – you should bet on Liz Kendall.'[1] Corbyn was initially estimated by bookkeepers to be a rank outsider, with 100–1 odds of winning, behind the favourite Andy Burnham, and the runners up Liz Kendall and Yvette Cooper.[2]

However, under the seemingly calm political surface, something was already stirring. There had been, in the wake of the Conservative victory, an angry reaction by Labour supporters, and a large anti-austerity march through central London attended by Corbyn. The Labour

establishment from which Burnham, Kendall and Cooper
were drawn had responded to the defeat by blaming
Miliband for being too left-wing. The 'Blue Labour' guru
Jon Cruddas fed mangled and misleading research to the
Guardian newspaper claiming to support this idea.[3] Such
claims were rejected by the British Election Study, which
pointed out that the major factor dogging Labour was the
2008 economic crash, Labour's version of the 1992 ERM
crisis.[4] But more importantly, they were rejected by a
growing number of Labour supporters. Labour's defeats
in the 1980s might have been blamed on the Left, but this
one was blamed firmly on the Right. As a result, Corbyn's
'dark horse' challenge had a certain momentum from the
beginning. Corbyn's early meetings were extremely well
attended, even if this fact was largely ignored by the media.

As the media belatedly began to pick up on 'Jeremy
Corbyn mania', with some bewilderment and alarm, high-
profile Labour figures including Tony Blair began to make
public statements, using their presumed moral authority
to warn against a gamble on Corbyn. The unease among
senior Labour figures was exacerbated by the decision
of major unions, such as Unite and Unison, to support
Corbyn – chiefly on the grounds that he was the only candidate to offer more than lukewarm opposition to the Tories'
planned anti-union legislation. The release of the first poll
for the leadership showing Corbyn with a serious lead over
all rivals prompted a slew of panicky and counterproductive interventions from Gordon Brown, Jack Straw, Alistair
Campbell and others.

What Blair, Brown, Straw, Campbell and the rest could

not understand was that for Corbyn's supporters, they were the very epitome of the problem, the right-wing establishment that they were rebelling against. Labour-supporting celebrities who rallied behind the mainstream candidates – for example, Steve Coogan's boasting about Andy Burnham's 'radical leftwing plan' for Britain[5] – also had little impact. Yet another poll was released, this one giving Corbyn a lead in the first round, with at least twenty points over his nearest rival. The panic from the Labour machine, as it sought to purge potential pro-Corbyn 'infiltrators', was matched by a public fear campaign from the likes of Labour MPs John Mann and Simon Danczuk, who demanded that the election be stopped, or that Corbyn be overthrown during his first days in office. Once again, this was counterproductive, since those who were likely to vote Corbyn were already convinced that the old leadership was undemocratic and didn't take members seriously.

With little support from any of the traditional media, Corbyn's campaign team turned to social media. Just as the UK Independence Party (UKIP) had exploited Twitter and Facebook to their advantage during the general election, even showing up the mainstream media to their supporters, Corbyn and his team were able to do the same. Through these means he built his mass meetings without recourse to the old media that were denying him due publicity, while the other candidates' meetings struggled to attract a dozen or so stragglers despite ample coverage. In the end, despite (and in part because of) the purges and fearmongering, Corbyn's victory was a first-round landslide, as he emerged with just under 60 per cent of the vote.

From Out of Nowhere

The story of Corbyn's challenge begins shortly after the 2015 general election. While the dominant narrative coming out of Labour's right-wing was that Labour had lurched to the unelectable left, a core of activists on the left were drawing very different conclusions. Few, when Corbyn first stood as a Labour leadership candidate, expected him to get on the ballot, much less stand a chance of winning. This was as much true of his close supporters and advisers as it was of his rivals. But there was a need to counter the Blairite narrative and create a space for an alternative point of view. The campaign's social media organiser and London regional organiser Marsha-Jane Thompson explains:

> We didn't think he had a chance of getting on the ballot paper. We had a strategy of holding regional meetings with figures like Owen Jones and Jon Trickett MP, publicising an alternative manifesto, explaining what we would say if Jeremy Corbyn did get on the ballot ... It was part of a wider anti-austerity initiative. There had been some good stuff in Ed Miliband's election manifesto which was downplayed by the right-wing, so our idea was to highlight the aspects of it that called for social justice and to highlight that there was a shift to the left there. We also wanted to challenge the Blairite narrative, which was that Labour lost because we had moved too far to the left. In fact, we lost because we didn't present a coherent alternative.[6]

Nevertheless, there was a sense quite early on that the situation was very different from that five years before, when the most left-wing candidate, John McDonnell MP, didn't even get on the ballot paper. Ben Sellers, a long-standing Labour activist and founder of *Red Labour*, recalls that while there was no guarantee that Corbyn would get on the ballot, there was a palpable current of discontent among party members:

> The grass roots was not particularly left-wing, but at the same time they were not happy with the cards they had been dealt by New Labour, or the exclusion of members from the decision-making process. They felt they were just there to do door-knocking, leaf-leting and so on. And even then, there was a controversy when the party started collecting data from door-knocking and gave people scripts, as if they couldn't cope with having conversations with people on the door-step. So there was a kickback against the lack of trust in the party membership. Then there were a hell of a lot of people keeping quiet, who you would see at People's Assembly events, but would never say they were in Labour, and for that reason weren't seen as the voice of the party. People thought the party was just full of Blairites, but the truth is, the Blairites were always a small minority in the party – they just happened to be the ones in positions of power in constituencies, or regional officials, or councillors. So, the left was silenced: they kept their paper member-ship, but they stopped going to meetings.[7]

For this discontent to be channelled into a leadership elec-tion process, however, there were some hoops to jump through. For all the talk of one-member-one-vote, the par-liamentary party still has a veto on who gets to stand for leader. Prior to 2014, a candidate had to have the support of at least 12.5 per cent of Labour MPs. After the implementation of reforms recommended in the Collins Review, the required level of support was increased to 15 per cent. This meant that Corbyn needed at least thirty-five nominations to even stand. Given that the dominant explanation in the party for its electoral defeat seemed to be that Ed Miliband was a recalcitrant socialist who dragged the party to the left, it was not obvious that MPs would give Corbyn the nominations he needed.

However, it was also glaringly apparent that without Corbyn the debate would be deathly dull and narrower than ever before. And there was a core group of activists with a degree of social media savvy, who were able to leverage the existing discontent in the party to put pressure on MPs to at least allow the debate to happen. Using Twitter, Facebook and email campaigns, they were able to build a momentum behind Corbyn's campaign that would not otherwise have existed. As Thompson put it:

> We sensed that this time it was different and they wouldn't be able to ignore us and sideline us as they historically had. The parliamentary party were under a lot of pressure from people who supported Jeremy's candidacy on social media ... One MP explained that she'd had a hundred constituents email her in one day demanding that Jeremy be admitted to the ballot.[8]

Newcastle MP Chi Onwurah explained on her website that she was nominating Corbyn not because she agreed with his policies but because 'I asked members and supporters in my constituency who I should nominate and the overwhelming feedback ... was that Jeremy Corbyn should be on the ballot.'[9] Some of those who welcomed Corbyn's candidacy did so the better to see his ideas clearly defeated. Labour activist Luke Akehurst explained, 'I want their ideas taken on democratically and defeated in an open contest of ideas.'[10] There was, in short, no expectation among his nominees or seasoned activists that Corbyn could win. But the mere fact that they were talking about him, in a way that they hadn't talked about previous campaigns mounted by John McDonnell, already suggested that something novel was happening. Corbyn squeezed past the nominations barrier at the last minute with just thirty-six nominees.

Some of the energies that would appear in the campaign began to make themselves visible in a significant public protest that summer. In June 2015, for the first time in several years, an anti-austerity protest drew tens of thousands of people to the streets. This would not have been the largest such protest if it had happened in 2011, the year of the Arab Uprisings, the Occupy movement and a series of mass demonstrations, public sector strikes and even riots in the UK. But on this occasion, it followed years of demoralisation and defeat, in which every crisis seemed to favour the Right. Labour's long retreat from its brief experiment with anti-austerity politics, its welfare-bashing and its feeble attempt to triangulate UKIP on immigration, had resulted in yet another election defeat. Labour's biggest problem, it had turned out, was motivating the younger electorate, who largely either did not turn out, or gave their votes to the Greens. Many of them now took to the streets and, as a major speaker at the concluding rally, Jeremy Corbyn set the direct and morally straightforward tone that would characterise his whole campaign. It was not a polished, rehearsed performance, and the candidate was not naturally charismatic. And far from sticking to the relatively easy critique of austerity, he made a point of defending the immigrants and 'welfare scroungers'[11] reviled both by Tories and previous Labour governments. From anyone else, a call for a 'kinder politics' would come across as a greasy, hypocritical shibboleth. In Corbyn's case, it was the core of his politics reduced to its simplest expression. He appealed for a new type of society where, 'we each care for all, everybody caring for everybody else: I think it's called socialism'.

This was only one crowd and far from the last of a series of large public events that Corbyn addressed. Soon, his meetings, held in cities across the country from Exeter to Newcastle, were as packed as those of his rivals were threadbare. But this one crowd in mid-June alone would have suggested that, if Corbyn could channel the discontent of Labour activists, he had the basis for a serious leadership challenge. As Stephen Bush wrote in the *New Statesman*, the size of the crowd in London – however exaggerated by organisers – pointed to the existence of a large enough activist base to win the Labour leadership:

> Let's say that just 10,000 of them can be convinced that the Labour Party, even one led by Corbyn, is worth the candle. Then they each need to recruit five friends. If just *one* of those five friends recruits another friend, Corbyn could be Labour's next leader.[12]

So it turned out. On one Saturday in August, Corbyn addressed 1,800 people in Manchester; 1,000 people in Derby; 1,700 in Sheffield's Crucible and a further 800 outside.[13] The patterns were repeated in Coventry, Plymouth, Liverpool, Birmingham and in London, where the Camden Centre was filled to bursting point with 2,000 people inside, and a crowd of several hundred outside. By the end of that month, it was announced that a total of 13,000 people had signed up to volunteer for his campaign. The daily growing list of celebrities supporting Corbyn in writing or in public events seemed to extend well beyond the list of 'usual suspects' who might be spotted at People's Assemblies – a motley cohort ranging from Emma Thompson and Daniel Radcliffe to Mary Beard and Lord Skidelsky. Labour membership soared wherever Corbyn touched down. In Colchester, following a meeting of over a thousand people, the biggest local political meeting for decades, the Labour Party membership quadrupled. The spectacle of thousands upon thousands of enthusiastic participants signing up to have anything to do with the Labour Party would have been unthinkable a few months before. The fact that there was a 'registered supporters' category also helped the Corbyn campaign team, since it gave them a chance to make a unique and compelling offer to those Leftists who were wary, on account of bitter experience, of joining Labour. As a senior advisor put it, 'the offer was, pay three quid and help smash Blairism for good. Many people would pay a lot more than that for such a privilege'. But while 100,000 people did sign up as registered supporters, almost twice that number, 183,658, signed up as full members. The number of new members alone was more than twice the membership of the Conservative Party.[14]

The campaign's ability to summon enthusiastic participation was matched by its online reach, and indeed the two aspects of the campaign were mutually supporting. Marsha-Jane Thompson recalls:

> There is a lot of exaggeration about social media, but we went from nothing to reaching 2.5 million people within four weeks of our Facebook page being launched. At the moment, our page reaches 11 million people every day … In Colchester, this meant that when we put the announcement out about our meeting on Facebook, all thousand tickets were gone within forty-five minutes. This was before the polls showed Corbyn leading the other candidates.[15]

In addition to organising meetings, the social media campaign was able to play off against negative media coverage, rebutting the scare stories, and also make a virtue of those aspects of Corbyn's ideology and career that the media would try to vilify. As Sellers explains,

> There were three strands to the social media campaign. There were the official [social media] accounts which consisted mainly of standard fare, official statements and so on. They grew huge, naturally. But there were also a number of semi-official accounts which we ran, where we had contact with press officers and people working on the ground in the offices in London, with whom we could discuss rebuttal strategies informally. We also had a slight distance from them. The campaign office didn't want to get involved in rebuttals, but we felt there were some things that needed to be taken on. So

we began to plug away at what Corbyn stood for, the fact that he had a consistent ideology, had remained principled since the 1980s, and we turned this into a positive. We simplified his messages and put them out in easily digestible formats, memes and stuff. Then there was a huge volume of people doing smaller projects that were nothing to do with us or even necessarily the Labour Party – pages like 'Kittens 4 Corbyn', and so on. We had some tangential contact with these pages, and we could discuss things with them now and again, but they actually did a lot of the rebuttal work off their own back.[16]

This is not a dynamic that is peculiar to the Left. It is part and parcel of a political scene in which the ideological monopoly of the traditional media is breaking down. With the rise of alternative sources of information – and according to YouGov, some 57 per cent of Corbyn's supporters received most of their information about the campaign from social media[17] – there is far less deference to the dominant television and press outlets than there had been before. Meanwhile, the antagonism of the news media to Corbyn tended to compound a sense among supporters of both the authenticity of the candidate, and the general untrustworthiness of the traditional media.

One of Corbyn's most important assets in the campaign was his ability to say exactly what he thought, and to express it in a straightforward idiom that anyone could grasp without insulting anyone's intelligence. This rapidly distinguished him from his rivals, who waffled and looked unconvincing when not delivering prepared remarks. There was, indeed, something unreal about their detachment,

their lack of direction, and their confusion in the face of
Corbyn's rising star. It didn't help their cause that there
were three candidates from the party's broad right-wing.
The Labour Right, and its media supporters, couldn't
agree on which of these to support. The *Mirror* backed
Andy Burnham, The *Guardian* supported Yvette Cooper
and the Tory press tended to favour Liz Kendall. The differences between the three candidates were miniscule,
but the fact that they all competed for the same shrink-
ing ideological space meant that there was no cohesive
opposition from the Labour Right to Corbyn's brand of
socialism.

It also didn't help that the candidates looked and sounded
like special advisors rather than political big-hitters. Jeremy
Gilbert, an associate at the soft-left group Compass,
recounts that at the inception of the New Labour project,
there was a clear divide between special advisors and the
loyal MPs parachuted in to safe seats,

> and the architects like Mandelson and Gould, who are more robust
> intellectually. But they could never persuade serious intellectuals or
> serious composite political organisers of their case, so they had to
> recruit banal and unthinking figures – and we saw the outcome of
> this in the leadership election.[18]

So, after years in government, ideologically and intellectually exhausted, divided into three candidates, the Right
faced Corbyn in a curiously hesitant mood. Sellers recalls
that 'they didn't talk a lot about policy, and they didn't challenge the policy stuff that we put out – in a way, we weren't

facing a serious opponent, which was odd. This wasn't the strong, efficient machine we were familiar with.'[19]

In a clip from LBC radio, which rapidly became viral, the four Labour candidates were asked by a member of the public to say whether Ed Miliband would feature in the shadow cabinet if they were elected. Corbyn gave a straight answer, in contrast to the waffling of the other candidates, prompting the host to remark: 'This is exactly why Jeremy Corbyn is shown in this *Times* poll this morning as way ahead of the rest of you, because he's given me a straight answer to a straight question, and the three of you can't do that.'[20] Participants at a typically packed meeting in Plymouth's Guildhall emphasised precisely that he spoke convincingly *as a Labour candidate*, in a way that none of his rivals did:

> 'He's saying things in a way that people can understand,' said Jo, a former secondary-school teacher. 'He says things that aren't pat-ronising, that are talking to working people, and that feel like what the grassroots of this party is all about,' she said. 'Change is the word,' said Kate Taylor, a feminist and Labour councillor who was elected at age eighteen, three years ago. 'I'm a bit sick of having to constantly put aside my own opinions and beliefs for the Labour Party. I would like to get the Labour Party back to what it was made to be, for working people,' she said.[21]

So it was that, as branch and union nominations began to come in, Corbyn was far ahead of his leadership rivals. Constituency Labour Parties had not been bulwarks of Leftism for some time, but here they gave Corbyn a clear advantage, with 152 constituency branches backing him. By contrast, 109 voted to support Yvette Cooper, 111 backed Andy Burnham and a humiliating 18 backed Liz Kendall. This should not be exaggerated: less than half of the branch nominations went to Corbyn, and he gained fractionally under half of the votes of full members in the final result. Yet no one expected a Left this vibrant in the Labour Party. The results suggested that a long dormant Left, the survivors of old and almost forgotten battles, had reanimated and fused with a younger generation radicalised through participation in social movements and single-issue campaigns.

Far more shockingly to the Labour establishment, Corbyn also gained the support of the largest trade unions, UNISON and Unite, as well as the endorsements of the postal workers union, the CWU, the transport workers' union, ASLEF, and the other transport workers' union, TSSA. Andy Burnham and Yvette Cooper divvied up the endorsements of the Musicians' Union, the depleted husk of the miners' union, the NUM, the builders' union, UCATT and the shop workers' union, USDAW. Liz Kendall gained no union endorsements. The advantage of having union support was that it meant there was a well-funded electoral machine working for Corbyn, which there simply hadn't been for previous left-wing leadership campaigns.

Why did the leaderships of the larger trade unions, which were not helmed by radical Leftists and had no history of supporting left-wing Labour leadership candidates, back Jeremy Corbyn in this instance? With few exceptions, such as the union backing for Tony Benn's deputy leadership campaign, the traditional stance of the trade unions in Labour's internal politics has been to support moderate leadership factions and equally moderate policies. It is true that since the election of a number of left-wing leaders dubbed 'the awkward squad', the general trend in trade union support has been to the left, but this has never before led to such a rift with the Labour Party establishment. It is also true that, of the range of alternative leadership candidates available to them, none would fight for union-backed policies in parliament in the way that Corbyn would. But the union leaders are accustomed to bargaining for minor concessions within the existing framework of the Labour Party, rather than, as they have done by supporting Corbyn, trying to fundamentally alter it.

In the case of UNISON's support, one could discern a pragmatic consideration. The threat of a looming election for general secretary Dave Prentis might have inclined him to think carefully about whether he could justify supporting any of the other candidates, none of whom supported union policy in the way that Corbyn did. And while that disciplinary pressure did not apply to any of the other unions, those involved in the Corbyn campaign could see other pressures at work. 'Union leaders are more connected to the grass roots than we give them credit for sometimes,' Thompson argues,

> and they could see which way their membership was going. They could see that members in their unions were signing up to support Jeremy. The data on their websites, where people could register to vote and back a candidate, showed that they were overwhelmingly backing Jeremy.[22]

Perhaps the most important consideration was hinted at in the CWU's official rationale for supporting Corbyn. They argued that Corbyn's victory would help break the 'grip of the Blairites ... once and for all'.[23] Throughout the whole period of Blairite dominance, the unions had been slowly sinking into an existential crisis. Their social depth has declined, the legislative climate has remained abysmal, industrial action has sunk to all-time lows, levels of manufacturing have continued to decline and the private sector is overwhelmingly non-unionised. Furthermore, the ability of the unions to do anything to reverse these trends has been seriously undermined by a series of reforms which have hacked away at their political clout within the Labour Party. The most recent of these was a package of measures recommended in the Collins Review, which in one manoeuvre disenfranchised millions of trade unionists. The spark for the reforms had been the Falkirk controversy, in which Unite was baselessly accused of rigging Labour's selection procedures. That Miliband instrumentalised this fake scandal in order to further weaken the union link ought to have put the unions on their guard. But, not wishing to embarrass Ed Miliband in the year before an election, and having been promised that the process would be continuously reviewed, they backed the reforms. This strategic blunder only compounded their crisis and it is likely that the victory of any other candidate would have led to their further marginalisation.

Corbyn's momentum, however much it enlivened the Labour Party, was met with a growing chorus of fury among Labour Rightists. As soon as it became clear that he was the favourite to win, with polls beginning to give him a clear lead as early as mid-July, panicked battle cries began to fly.

'Project Fear'

During the campaigns for and against Scottish independence, the leadership of the Unionist 'Better Together' campaign comprising both Labour and Conservative parties embarked on an offensive privately dubbed 'Project Fear' by the organisers.[24] The idea was, rather than selling the benefits of the Union, to terrify Scottish voters with visions of political and economic chaos should they vote to leave the UK. At its peak, Project Fear brought together leading figures in the state, business and media operators. The *Financial Times* reported[25] that the government twisted the arms of business leaders – 85 per cent of whom supported the Union – to go public with a series of warnings about economic disaster in the event of independence. Meanwhile, the civil service abandoned its customary pretence of neutrality, as the head of the Treasury Sir Nicholas Macpherson argued that there was no need for neutrality when 'the very existence of the British state was at stake'. Sir Jeremy Heywood, the cabinet secretary, drafted the Queen's intervention in the debate, while the Treasury published unusually partisan advice. Research showed that the main broadcast media, above all the BBC, were on board with the fear campaign, overwhelmingly publicising negative claims about independence.[26]

A remarkably similar pattern was to emerge in the case

of the Left's capture of the Labour leadership. During the leadership election, three Labour MPs from the party's right-wing – John Mann, Barry Sheerman and Graham Stringer – called for the process to be halted, claiming to be worried about infiltration by the far Left and Tory trolls.[27] They argued that the new rules under which the election was being conducted made it impossible to vet participants. As Stringer put it, with the influx of registered support-ers, 'We do not know and could never know whether these people support other political parties.' Sheerman likewise contended that among infiltrators, only a few of the 'usual suspects' could possibly be detected by vetting measures. Mann suggested that 'long-standing members' might be 'trumped by people who have opposed the Labour Party', invoking the danger of a return of the old Trotskyist faction, Militant.

The *Sunday Times* joined in, leading the charge with a front-page story amplifying calls for Harriet Harman to cancel the leadership vote: 'Hard left plot to infiltrate Labour race.'[28] The only solid evidence of such a plot was a call by a groupuscule called the Communist Party of Great Britain for members to join Labour and support Corbyn. This was a group whose membership didn't exceed two dozen, and whose major claim to fame was its weekly news-sheet, recognised among the cognoscenti as the *Heat* magazine of the far Left. Otherwise it rested entirely on over-heated claims by right-wing Labour MPs and anony-mous officials. Nonetheless, the piece succeeded in framing Corbyn's supporters as a deviant demographic, a trope that persists in the punditry of the traditional media. Dan

Hodges, a Blairite pundit and former spin doctor who had complained about Corbyn even making it onto the ballot, evoked a distorted image of Labour Party constituency meetings swarming with 'dozens of proto-Trotskyists ... demanding a people's revolution, and shouting down anyone who disagrees with taunts of "Red Tory"'.[29] Andy McSmith, a journalist sympathetic to the Labour Right, was less excited about infiltration plots, yet he too rather sneeringly characterised Labour's registered supporters as '£3 day trippers whose idea of political involvement is to log on, vote Corbyn, and tell your mates via Facebook'.[30]

In fact, the rules that these people now complained about were exactly the same rules as had been approved overwhelmingly by conference, with 86 per cent of the vote and with opposition largely coming from the Left, in the year before the leadership election.[31] They were part of the wider series of transformations recommended in the Collins Review, which weakened the union link and were welcomed at the time as a radicalisation and deepening of previous Blairite reforms.[32] The logic of such reforms was to achieve a transformation that even Blair could not. Labour, at its inception, federated the institutions of the labour movement into a broad political party, with trade unionists making up the organised core. The New Labour project had been, in part, to replace this federal structure with one in which the organised core was the professional strata that ran the party, while the base consisted exclusively of individualised supporters and members. By weakening the union link, and replacing the levy-paying trade unionists with a mass of largely passive supporters paying a small fee, the party would be anchored firmly in the political centre.

What Labour's party managers had sought, ironically, was precisely the political day tripper – a cash cow, and voting fodder, but otherwise not likely to make life difficult for the party professionals. If no one at the time worried about the possibility of Trotskyist infiltration, this was because it would make precious little difference to anything even if it did happen. That analysis still holds. Almost 300,000 people signed up as members and registered supporters of the Labour Party during the election campaign. The total weight of the far Left in the UK is, based on the acknowledged (and often exaggerated) memberships of its organisations, less than 5 per cent of that total. What is more, most of its members wouldn't be seen dead in Labour – indeed, many of them have spent years eagerly working to replace it with a British equivalent of the Continent's radical Left parties.

Yet, rather than clearsightedly dismissing most of these largely confected complaints of infiltration, the Labour Party management decided to act on them, and began a process of purges. In doing so, they took a fairly broad interpretation of their remit, purging for example the general secretary of the civil servants' union, the PCS, Mark Serwotka. It is not clear how many were excluded in total. Some alarmist reports, apparently encouraged by acting leader Harriet Harman, who talked up the number of supposed 'infiltrators', gave the impression that up to 100,000 people might be purged. The total number of people expelled by the end of the process was reportedly closer to

3,000. Many of those who were banned were targeted for having previously been members or supporters of other centre-left parties such as the Greens. The perfect idiocy of this defies measurement. For most young political activists, in an era when party identifications are weaker than they have ever been, and when the electoral system is showing signs of unusual volatility, a degree of political polyamory should be expected. It would be remarkable, and something Labour should regret, if it were unable to win back those who might have dallied in the past with the Liberals, the Greens or the Scottish National Party (SNP) – and odd for a party that used to proudly brag about former Tory MPs it had lured into the Blairite fold. To react to success on this front as evidence of 'infiltration', when the party managers know perfectly well that there is no evidence of organised entryism, bespeaks some form of political derangement. Worse, many of those whom were expelled were not driven out for anything as substantive as an impure political past. The party simply had 'reason to believe' that they did 'not support the aims and values of the Labour Party'. These and similar expulsions appear to have been based on vexatious complaints emailed from local constituency chairs eager to ward off the Corbynite offensive.[33]

While the Labour Party machinery experimented with excluding party members and supporters on the basis of near-Jesuitical distinctions, the media dutifully advised the public of the coming danger. The near-unanimity of the media's offensive, supported by the Conservative Party, a section of the Labour Right and actors within the state, was hard to miss. The Media Reform Coalition, set up in

the wake of 'Hackgate' – the infamous scandal exposing
News of the World phone-hacking and the shady relationship of the Murdoch press to top politicians and police
chiefs – studied the press response to Corbyn's victory and
found that the papers 'systematically undermined' Corbyn
from the first day of his leadership. A survey of 494 articles
across the press found that 60 per cent of the coverage was
negative, with only 13 per cent positive.[34]

The right-wing newspapers predictably augured 'chaos'.
The *Telegraph* predicted that union leaders would try to
use 'coordinated strikes and demonstrations' to 'topple the
Government', while another columnist warned of Corbyn's
supporters 'seizing the means of production and distribution directly through strikes and organised demands'.[35]
The *Daily Mail* published a delirious fantasy about Jeremy
Corbyn taking office and the first days of his administration, which began: 'The night sky over London was thick
with choking black smoke…'.[36] Invoking an indebted
basket-case economy torn apart by rioters, demonstrators
and revolutionaries, it was practically salivating over the
apocalyptic scenario it conjured up. One can't help but see
in such eristic a degree of projection and nostalgic wish-
fulfilment: the right-wing yearning for the old fighting
days of the Cold War, when they could crush the Left in the
name of the Free World. Even the seemingly sober *Financial
Times* was at it, complaining of an 'air of menace' stalk-
ing Corbyn's campaign: 'National socialism, it was once
called. One side waves the flag, the other demands a bigger
state. Both rail against outsiders – the right against immigrants, the left against international capitalism.'[37] Here, the

exuberant followers of a bearded, anti-war socialist were found to be analogous to the Third Reich. The *Financial Times* not only reached the threshold of Godwin's Law, in three sentences, it also compared powerful multinational capital to the desperate refugees being left to drown in the Mediterranean and subject to racist persecution across Europe.

One of the most insidious attacks from the Right was organised by the *Jewish Chronicle*, edited since 2008 by the Tony Blair-worshipping neoconservative pundit Stephen Pollard. In an article published a month before the outcome, the *Chronicle* posed a series of 'key questions Jeremy Corbyn must answer'.[38] Most of these were insinuation, guilt-by-association tactics. So, for example, it queried his links to Carlos Latuff, whom it characterised as 'the notorious anti-Semitic cartoonist'. Latuff is notoriously pro-Palestinian, but support for Palestine is a far cry from anti-Semitism. Even the Jewish daily *Forward* considers it a 'stretch' to call his cartoons 'antisemitic'.[39] Far more insidious was the attack on Corbyn for supporting Raed Salah, whom the *Chronicle* depicted as 'a man convicted of the blood libel'. This was particularly obnoxious, because Salah had been the subject of a deportation struggle, in which these claims of anti-Semitism were used by the government to support his expulsion from the UK. What the *Chronicle* failed to mention was that Salah won that court case precisely because these claims were shown to be false and based on mistranslations.[40] The fact that Salah was being slandered by the government is the reason why Corbyn, quite ethically, stood by him. Nonetheless, the *Chronicle*'s article provided material for reams and reams of similarly insinuating media attacks, such as Dan Hodges's claim that Corbyn's victory would be 'cheered by terrorists and racists'; and it served as ammunition for Labour's mayoral candidate Sadiq Khan to attack Corbyn in the *Daily Mail* for 'encouraging' terrorism.[41]

The centre-left press had its own lines of attack. The *Guardian*, a long-standing ally of the Labour Right, played a particularly shoddy role, both in its journalism and its comment pages. Its comment pages were filled with condescension toward Corbyn and his supporters from comment editor Jonathan Freedland, leader writer Anne Perkins, columnist Suzanne Moore (a former eurocommunist pugilist from the pages of *Marxism Today*) and veteran columnist Martin Kettle (another former *Marxism Today* writer) – all essentially repeating the habitual refrain of Corbyn's Labour critics that he and his supporters were obsessed with their narrow concerns and oblivious to his unelectability.[42] Its sister paper, the *Observer*, was little different, with senior journalist Andrew Rawnsley deriding Corbyn's 'promised land', belittling its 'fantasy' politics and invoking Labour's 'near-destruction at the hands of the Bennites'.[43] The paper's editorial repudiating Corbyn finally induced an exasperated response from the *Observer*'s senior journalist Ed Vulliamy, who wondered why the paper had joined in the chorus of attacks, leaving 'a lot of good, loyal and decent people who read our newspaper feeling betrayed'.[44] Symptomatically, the flood of disobliging column inches about Jeremy Corbyn in these newspapers was marked by constant harking back to the 1980s. As if nothing fundamental had changed that might bear thinking about. As if the same battles could be re-staged – and indeed, the *Guardian* gave space to one of Labour's wealthiest donors to suggest that a Corbyn victory could be met by an SDP-style split.[45] As if those rallying to Corbyn might not be responding to the problems of twenty-first-century Britain. As if part of the problem might not be the palpable inadequacy of the candidates whom liberal commentators seemed to think had a right to win, regardless of the paucity of their campaigns. One is entitled to wonder who it is here who was really stuck in the past, and really mired in self-serving fantasy.

One of the main methods of obloquy from the centre-left papers – aside from the claim that Corbyn's supporters were either spaniel-eyed naïfs, gently prancing around in cloud cuckoo land, or dangerous ideological zealots – was to bait Corbyn's supporters as sexist. The *Guardian* had backed Yvette Cooper for the leadership, partially on the grounds that she would be the first female leader, bringing 'down-to-earth feminism' to the role, and challenging austerity policies that hurt women. Its leading columnist and former Social Democratic Party (SDP) star Polly Toynbee seconded the endorsement, announcing: 'Labour needs a woman leader.'[46] This prompted a reply by the seasoned feminists Selma James and Nina Lopez, who pointed out that Cooper not only supported 'sexist austerity' but had also implemented it in government, abolishing income support and extending work-capability assessments for the sick and disabled.[47] Nonetheless, having supported Cooper as a 'feminist', it didn't require much imagination to notice

that Corbyn was not female and thus to indict his supporters 'brocialists'. Suzanne Moore complained that as Corbyn
was 'anointed leader' — that is to say, elected leader — 'not
one female voice was heard'.[48] The remarkable thing about
this complaint was that Corbyn won among women by a
landslide. The polls showed that 61 per cent of women eli-
gible to vote in the election supported Corbyn, while the
two female candidates, Liz Kendall and Yvette Cooper,
gained 4 per cent and 19 per cent respectively. The polling
company YouGov pointed out that 'women who are eli-
gible to vote are dramatically more likely to vote Corbyn
than men'.[49] What Moore meant was that she hadn't lis-
tened to the women who supported Corbyn, an important
distinction.

This campaign spread to the *Independent*, which published a surreal piece headlined, 'If it's truly progressive,
Labour will have voted in a female leader — regardless of
her policies'.[50] It was also mirrored in the *Telegraph*, which
gleefully wondered if Corbyn had a 'women problem'.[51]
Cathy Newman, a *Channel 4 News* reporter who had
recently made headlines by falsely reporting an example
of sexist exclusion at a mosque, authored a piece for the
Telegraph which sneered: 'Welcome to Jeremy Corbyn's
blokey Britain — where "brocialism" rules'.[52] Newman's
complaint did not concern policy, on which Corbyn was
difficult to attack, but representation. She alleged that none
of the 'top jobs' went to women. Corbyn's shadow cabinet,
it must be said, was notable for being the first to have
more than 50 per cent of its posts occupied by women[53] —
as opposed to the pathetic 22 per cent representation that

women have in wider public life. The shadow ministries of Defence, Business, Health, and Education were all run by women. The shadow cabinet was, in other words, more gender-egalitarian on this front than any previous Labour shadow cabinet. It is perfectly fair comment to lament that important posts such as shadow chancellor have never been held by a woman, but the force of the point is blunted if it is simply used in an opportunistic way to belabour Corbyn. Likewise, the *New Statesman*'s effort to pour cold water on Corbyn's victory, with the headline 'Labour chooses white man as leader', would have been far more convincing if the publication had not generously supported every previous white man elected as Labour leader.[54]

Another major theme of the ongoing campaign was Corbyn's supposed unelectability. A typical example of this was the *Independent*'s misleading story, originally accompanied by a false headline that read: 'Jeremy Corbyn "loses a fifth of Labour voters"'.[55] The substance of the story, carefully obscured within prevaricating formulations, showed something completely different. Sixty-three per cent of Labour voters said they were more likely to vote Labour in the next election with Corbyn as leader, as opposed to 20 per cent who said they were more likely to vote Conservative. Over a third of SNP voters, approximately a third of Liberal Democrats, about one-fifth of UKIP voters and 8 per cent of Tories were more likely to vote Labour with Corbyn as Labour leader. And four-fifths of Tory voters were more determined to vote for their own party, just under a fifth of SNP voters would be more likely to vote Tory, while a third of Liberals and 40 per cent of UKIPers would be more likely to vote Conservative. Corbyn had not lost voters: he had polarised them in a new way.

The class valence of Corbyn's supposed unelectability varied, depending on whom one was listening to. According to an opinion piece in the *Telegraph*, Corbyn's 'sub-Marxist drivel' showed that he had 'no understanding of the British people',[56] whose great middle class had no need of the types of Leftist reforms he proposed. A similarly splenetic piece in the *Guardian* held that Corbyn's Labour was so 'poncified' that working-class voters had turned off in droves.[57] These claims reached a comical zenith during an otherwise unremarkable by-election. The *Times* had insisted that Labour was 'counting the cost' of Corbyn's peacenik antics in Oldham, where a UKIP challenge was ready to reduce Labour's majority to a margin of error.[58] John Harris, in a video report from Oldham for the *Guardian*, held that 'Corbynmania' was about to collide with 'reality'.[59] Corbyn's leadership was 'looking increasingly fragile', Harris averred, and cited an encounter with an anti-Corbyn Labour voter to suggest that perhaps the only remaining Labour voters would be the hardened tribalists who put the party first. There being no polling in this by-election, journalists relied on a combination of anecdotes, vox pops and their own prejudices. In the end, Labour held the seat not only with a sizeable majority of over ten thousand, but increased its share of the vote with a 7.5 per cent swing in its favour. The anticlimax was palpable, and the *Telegraph* wondered whether 'Muslims worried about war' might not be to blame for the victory.[60]

Other hit pieces strained for effect. For example, a story in the *Telegraph* – a paper that, more than any other, has been out for Corbyn's blood – referred to claims that Corbyn had a consensual relationship with Diane Abbot in the late 1970s as 'damaging'.[61] Janet Daley of the *Telegraph* recounted a horror story from Haringey in the seventies in which Jeremy Corbyn, as a local councillor, may or may not have been indifferent to the squatters residing in a house next to hers.[62] Anne Perkins of the *Guardian*, with a tone so stiff as to be almost beyond satire, complained that Corbyn had not sang the national anthem at a commemoration service: 'it is his job to sing it'.[63] The *Sun* published a false story alleging that Jeremy Corbyn was a 'hypocrite' since, as a republican, he was willing to bend his knee and kiss the Queen's hand in order to secure state funds for Labour.[64] This was complemented by another *Sun* 'scoop', claiming, again falsely, that Corbyn 'refused to bow' to the Queen, in an apparently trivial defiance of protocol.[65] Such contradictory characterisations suggested something of an internal conflict in the smear department: was Corbyn an inflexibly, excessively principled left-winger, or a conniving opportunist? This dreary sequence of contrived stories reached peak absurdity with the media's extraordinary attention to Corbyn's precise comportment in the laying of a wreath at the Cenotaph, with piece after piece suggesting that his solemn nod of the head was not quite solemn enough.[66]

As the government prepared for war in Syria, and Corbyn tried to rally his MPs to oppose it, pro-war Labour MPs continued to generate tittle-tattle for the press. For example, as the parliamentary vote neared, these seasoned

warriors – closets groaning with skeletons, minds keenly
attuned to the location of buried bodies – suddenly discovered an extraordinarily delicate temper when faced with
criticism, online or offline. News reports listed examples of
'bullying' and 'intimidation' of pro-war MPs, such as protesters gathering outside the constituency office of Peter
Kyle MP; an email sent to Labour MPs by someone claiming to be a Labour Party member to the effect that, if they
voted for war, they would face votes of no confidence in
their constituencies; a Labour councillor suggesting that
MPs who voted for war should face re-selection ballots;
a tweet sent to Stella Creasy pointing out that 'in the
digital age there is a lot more accountability to voters';
Labour MPs being called mean things such as 'war-
monger', and 'red Tory'; and finally, in December 2015,
a news story emerged, based on social media rumours,
that anti-war protesters had marched past Stella Creasy
MP's home. As it transpired, the story was wholly untrue,
but it provoked a series of denunciations of 'bullying',
and calls from Deputy Leader Tom Watson to expel any
Labour members who were found to have participated.[67]
A perverse logic thus unfolded, in which Labour MPs,
claiming to be victimised, bullied and threatened with ex-
communication, demanded that activists with whose politics they disagreed be victimised, bullied and purged.
Without evidence to support their case, MPs launched a
campaign to force Corbyn to disband the nascent Labour
left group Momentum. They were not able to inculpate the
group in any bullying, but feebly suggested that some of
its members probably were involved – and thus the leader

of the Labour Party should act with monarchical haste to crush the insurgents.[68]

These frivolities were interwoven with another, ongoing line of attack. The Tories had responded to Corbyn's victory with a series of messages and social media memes designed to identify Corbyn as a threat to 'national security' – or, less euphemistically, as an anti-British weirdo who doesn't know how to bow properly at the Cenotaph, won't sing the national anthem, will not (or, nefariously, will) kiss the Queen's hand, and has a romantic affiliation to the nation's enemies. Characteristic of this obnoxious campaign was a *Telegraph* piece by Tory MP and former soldier Tom Tugenhat, who expostulated that Corbyn was a terrorist ally who 'wants to see Britain defeated'.[69] But far more alarming were the interventions by the military leadership in this debate. The first came via the *Sunday Times*, which published without comment or criticism the statements of an unnamed senior army general who claimed that a Corbyn government, if it abandoned Trident and cut military spending, could be subject to an armed forces mutiny.[70] The fact that this was not widely regarded in media or Westminster circles as an outrageous attack on democracy, suggested that at least some of the British media was prepared to take a positively Venezuelan turn, allowing itself to become a mouthpiece for the most belligerent elements of the anti-Corbyn chorus. Later, as the campaign over Trident heated up, the chief of staff of the British armed forces used an appearance on the BBC to state that he would be worried if Corbyn's views were 'translated into power'. This was an explicit and probably planned breach of neutrality, but more notably it was then defended by Corbyn's own shadow defence secretary, whose differences with Corbyn on Trident had been made clear. No discipline was applied to the chief of staff.[71]

Here, then, were all the classic ingredients of a 'Project Fear' campaign: a toxic combination of falsehoods, insinuation, trivialisation, scaremongering, and pointed political interventions by the supposedly neutral apparatuses of the state. By and large, it did not work. This is not to say that it went without benefit for those undertaking it. Corbyn would have to struggle under any circumstances to define a radical agenda that would work in modern Britain, win the media battles to gain a voice for his objectives and assemble a viable electoral coalition behind it. In the context of 'Project Fear', he and his allies have had to navigate an almost daily sequence of contrived outrages, neutralise hundreds of petty but toxic talking points, and continually negotiate a truce with his own back benchers. Yet Corbyn won by a mile and remains in the leadership with the overwhelming support of the party membership. Despite dire predictions, there has not been a crash in the Labour vote, although it has not markedly improved either. The fact that Corbyn's opponents have been unsuccessful thus far suggests that there's something they're missing.

The Rage of the Labour Right

Adam Phillips suggests that our rages disclose what it is we think we are entitled to. We become infuriated when the world doesn't live up to our largely unconscious assumptions about how it should be for us. What might the fury of Labour's right-wingers, as well as their media allies, tell us about their entitlement? Their denial about the depths of Corbyn's support within Labour, their seeming belief that they have a right to be safeguarded against the critical and sometimes harsh words of activists, not to mention against the mere suggestion that they may at some point be answerable to members for their actions, all suggests an almost proprietorial attitude to the party.

They, of course, prefer to see their efforts as an attempt to spare the party electoral oblivion. Labour had lost the 2015 election, as a prominent former advisor to Tony Blair claimed, because it was led by an incompetent left-winger.[72] There was always something about this that smacked of wishful thinking: as if the problems facing the Labour Party were reducible to an easily rectifiable political deviation. In fact, as the right-wing commentator Tim Stanley acknowledged,

> we live in a post-Cold War world where both Left and Right have already triangulated towards a narrow middle. The Left has swerved far, far to the Right. Labour has dumped nationalisation, industrial democracy, pacifism and socialist internationalism. Given this fact, I fail to buy the argument that only by moving dramatically Rightward can the party become competitive.[73]

Nonetheless, the logic is clear. If Labour had swung too far to the left, how could electing the most left-wing leader in the party's history possibly be the solution? In fact, it is evident that for many of Corbyn's opponents in the Labour

Party, even if he *was* the solution, they would rather not resuscitate the party in that way. As Tony Blair put it with refreshing candour, 'I wouldn't want to win on an old-fashioned leftist platform. Even if I thought it was the route to victory, I wouldn't take it.'[74]

Blair's case is exactly as it has always been. In the name of modernity and its outward manifestations – globalisation, technological innovation, 'change' – Labour must abandon the shibboleths of 'the past', and learn to govern a twenty-first-century society. It must accept markets and harness them, rather than attempting to control them. A party which tries to govern on any other basis is destined for the charnel house. Given this, it is not just a matter of thinking that Corbyn can't win for Labour, but also of hoping that he never does.

And indeed, as one of Blair's ideological comrades, Dan Hodges, wrote in the Tory-supporting *Telegraph*, Labour 'moderates' were confessing that they wanted the party to lose under Corbyn:

> 'It's crazy,' one Labour MP confides to me. 'The decent people of my constituency and I have to act out this charade. We keep talking to each other about fighting hard for [Labour mayoral candidate Sadiq Khan], and secretly we're all thinking, "But I hope he loses."'[75]

This chronicles the evolution of the positions of Labour's right-wing zealots. First, the Left can't win. Second, it shouldn't win. And third, it would be better to crash Labour than to let it win under a left-wing leadership. It is one small step from this reasoning to outright defection. Here, the

Blairites are a little more cautious. While some are more or less open in calling for a split,[76] there appears to be a general recognition for now that this can't work. Polly Toynbee, a veteran SDP splitter, warns that it would fail: 'Unlike Foot, Corbyn has compromised on Europe and Nato, so there is no single break point.'[77] John Rentoul, Blair's biographer and a vitriolic opponent of the Left, argues,

> The conditions for a new centre-left party are less favourable than they were when the Social Democratic Party was launched in 1981 – then, the Conservatives had moved to the right while the London liberal middle class and the media were all for a new party.[78]

The fact that the historical spectre of the SDP is even raised in this context is indicative of the scale of alarm on the Labour Right. One does not, in the context of the Labour Party, so nakedly dispense with the 'broad church' rhetoric and openly dally with the idea of desertion, unless one is scared out of one's wits. The party's right-wing has usually found the 'broad church' trope a convenient one, dignifying its grip on power and its marginalisation of the Left. And it has long benefited immensely from the matchless tribalism of party culture.

After all, 'everyone knows' – and not wholly without reason – that the SDP split confirmed Thatcher in power for the rest of the 1980s. Breaking up the traditional Labourist electoral coalition into two jagged fractions – middle-class liberals on one side, and the working-class Left on the other – they handed the Tories an indestructible parliamentary majority with which to annihilate one quarter of Leftist potency after another. This is engrained into Labour's folk memory.

The Blairites have to be panicking to talk like this – and panic they might. They can handle their party losing electoral appeal. Labour shed some 5 million votes, largely from the working-class heartlands, between 1997 and 2010. They can handle being unpopular on major policy issues. Blair was happy to campaign in 2001 on the flagship policy of Private Finance Initiatives, though they were opposed by some 80 per cent of the public, and later staked his leadership on the invasion of Iraq. They can even stand to be out of power in their own party for some time. Ed Miliband's leadership was not the one the Blairites had sought, yet they did not panic.

What they are now panicking about is that, whereas Miliband at least shared the Blairites' axioms for judging success or failure, Corbyn does not. As the BBC's Mark Mardell put it,

> Journalists and politicians based at Westminster ... measure daily success and failure through a set of unwritten rules reached by instinct rather than reflection ... It is often about a tug of war between positive and negative headlines, trials of strength over internal and external opponents, with all the fragility of narrative within a bubble. One of the reasons Mr Corbyn attracts so much opprobrium from those whose orbit circles planet Westminster is he will not accept their measure of his worth.[79]

Meanwhile, their fetishes are being turned against them. New Labour once idolised modernity, its slick, Britpop-friendly electoral mercenaries extolling the virtues of novelty and change, however vapidly, at every opportunity. Now they appear every bit as dated as Britpop; or as the Oasis frontman Noel Gallagher, whose valiant defence of Blairism raised a universal shrug.[80] The 'modernisation' demanded by Labour's millennials and its post-credit crunch supporters has little to do with focus groups and courting Rupert Murdoch.

One can hardly blame Labour's 'moderates' for feeling aggrieved. By their own standards, they achieved an outstanding success. The litany, usually delivered in staccato sentences, is by now well-worn. A national minimum wage. Investment in public services. A raft of new mechanisms to deliver 'social inclusion'. Ambitious measures to combat rough-sleeping and child poverty. A more tolerant society, with gay rights widely accepted. Again and again, New Labour intellectuals insist, Blair and Brown shaped an agenda that their opponents were forced to accept. They built a ruthless, powerful electoral machine that secured 'hegemony' and changed Britain for the better. The Tories were excluded from office for three terms until they finally abandoned an unavailing neo-Thatcherite path, and chose a liberal leadership. Though the New Labour intelligentsia would never put it like this, Cameron was as much Blair's legacy as Blair was Thatcher's achievement.

Meanwhile, they assert, the current Labour leadership will overreach and achieve nothing. However legitimate the indictment of austerity politics and inequality, they insist, Corbyn simply can't win power. Blair's strategist,

Peter Hyman, argues that a left-wing party of the sort that Corbyn would like to lead,

> could gain the support of 15 per cent to 20 per cent of the public and possibly, with the infrastructure, money and backing of the big trade unions, up to 25 per cent to 28 per cent of the vote. Let's not forget Michael Foot's Labour party got 27.6 per cent of the vote in 1983. But this is a party that will never be in power.[81]

At most, the Blairites claim, a Labour Party led from the left can expect to win some arguments, but it can't win elections; it will never dominate the conversation, or lead, because its social basis is too narrow. Is there anything to this argument? There could be, if the Corbyn leadership only sought to represent its own core support. Jeremy Gilbert of Compass points out:

> Corbyn rallied the metropolitan left vote: not just in London, but in the other big cities. This represents consistently about 25 per cent of the electorate, and they now demand representation. The assumption that the hard-Left represents only a negligible minority is wrong; they didn't disappear. A quarter of the public, if you look at the British Social Attitudes Surveys, are socialists, whereas about 8 to 15 per cent are fascists. It's interesting to think about why that is invisible and what it implies about the hegemony of liberalism in the media.[82]

Corbyn, then, has a base, but just not enough to win an election by itself. The 'moderate' case, then, is that Labour has to choose between being a left-wing organisation, and being an electorally successful organisation. And, as Peter Mandelson reminded the Blairite faithful in a 'leaked' memo written after Corbyn's success, 'electability remains the party's founding purpose from when the trade unions first created the Labour Representation Committee. If we cannot represent people in parliament and government what is the point of the party?'[83] There is something to all of this. Labour is an electoralist organisation first and foremost, and always has been. And winning elections does mean building coalitions, since the core vote is never enough. The problem for the 'moderates' is this: they aren't actually anywhere near as good at winning elections as they like to think.

Even in their reputed 'golden age', beginning in the bright summer of 1997, New Labour was the beneficiary of timing and fortune far more than of the strategic genius of Mandelson and company. The Tories had already decisively lost the support of a stratum of 'secular' voters who tend to vote with their wallets. Any general election held after the 1992 ERM crisis would have been Labour's to lose.[84] (Admittedly, that is no surety that they would not have lost it; Mandelson's savvy did not prevent the loss of the 1992 election.) New Labour's first term in office, between 1997 and 2001, saw their electoral coalition shrink by 3 million voters, largely from the poorest parts of the country. Were it not for the ongoing crisis wracking the Conservative Party, and the oddities of Britain's electoral system – two factors over which electoral gurus and spinners had little control – such a haemorrhaging of support could have been fatal, leaving Blair another one-term Labour Prime Minister.

Blair's third general election victory in 2005 was obtained with just over a third of the popular vote, and a total number of votes (9.5 million) similar to that achieved by Ed Miliband (9.35 million) in the disastrous 2015 election, in which Labour finally lost the entirety of Scotland. What was the big difference between a record third election victory and a crushing defeat? The revival of the Conservative vote. The Tories had undergone a detox operation, with a youthful, glabrous-cheeked leader doing his best Blair imitation. The deranged Right had largely decamped to UKIP. A period in coalition government with the Liberals had persuaded middle-ground voters that the Tories were no longer dominated by rancorous flag-wavers and pound-savers. (One might add, since it has become a psephological commonplace, that the credit crunch was 'Labour's ERM crisis', but this is only partially true: Labour decisively lost this argument in retrospect, and it was by no means inevitable that they should have done so.)

What about today? Whatever they think of Corbyn's electoral chances, the Blairites own electoral prospects are not necessarily better. Polls taken of the prospective Labour candidates before the leadership election found that of all the candidates, Corbyn was the favourite.[85] The 'moderates', lacking an appealing message, were also about as charismatic as lavatory soap dispensers. Labour's poll ratings under Corbyn are poor, but hardly worse than before despite the ongoing media feeding frenzy. There is no reason to believe that any of his lacklustre rivals would be doing any better than Corbyn presently is.

Why might this be, and why have the pundits been so

easily impressed by the claims of Labour's right-wing? Thinking through the electoral arithmetic on the Blairites' own terms, it was never obvious that the electoral bloc comprising people who think the same way as they do is even close to 25 per cent. The reason this hasn't been a problem in the past is that elections in Britain's first-past-the-post system are usually decided by a few hundred thousand 'median' voters based in marginal constituencies. As long as Labour could take the votes of the Left for granted, they could focus on serenading the 'aspirational' voters of Nuneaton. Even the erosion of 'heartland' votes didn't register, so long as this erosion was happening to mountainous, seemingly unassailable majorities.

What happens, however, when left-leaning electors defect in sufficient numbers and sufficient geographic concentration to pose serious questions about Labour's medium-term survival? What happens when it is no longer just the odd Labour seat going to George Galloway or Caroline Lucas in sudden unpredictable surges, but the whole of Scotland being lost in a single bloodbath? What happens when votes for left-of-centre rivals surge (the SNP vote trebling, the Green vote quadrupling), millions of potential voters still stay at home, and all of this takes place while the Conservatives reconstitute themselves as a viable centre-right governing party? This is one of the reasons why Corbynism has emerged in the first place: in that circumstance, Blairite triangulation turns out to be as useful as a paper umbrella, only any good until it starts raining.

This Is Not 1981

In the last analysis, Corbyn's victory was decisively enabled not by organisational changes or by 'infiltration'. Nor was it a result of the dynamism of the Left. In a way, the Left punched well above its real weight to secure this victory. Corbyn won because the Labour Party was weak, and the traditionally dominant party ideologies, and the normally effective modes of political control, had broken down. At the core of this was the degeneration of the union link, which had been hacked away at over years, with the result that the traditionally cautious union bureaucracies seized on a drastic opportunity to reverse their losses. The intellectual and ideological enervation both of the New Labour project and of those who had governed as New Labour ministers, meant that Corbyn was able to answer the existential questions posed about Labour's future far more convincingly than any of his rivals.

It is the denial of this state of affairs that lies behind the fantasy of Labour's Right that the party's problems will only be solved by re-enacting the battles of the 1980s. Faced with the Corbyn ascendancy, some seasoned Labour Rightists have reacted with familiar relish. Roy Hattersley, who had spent years ineffectually bemoaning the Blairites, suddenly seems to have recovered his élan. Recounting his travails in right-wing Labour politics in the early eighties, he exhorts Labour 'moderates' to take the battle to Corbyn in the spirit of Denis Healey. The battle must be fought 'all over again', he declaims. 'The sooner the fightback begins the better.'[86] But anyone looking for Cold War reheats in this manner is wasting their time.

There are a number of reasons that Hattersley, Healey and other hammers-of-the-Left were able to defeat the Left in the early-to-mid-eighties which simply don't obtain today. One is that the wider climate of opinion was moving sharply to the right at the time, while the Left – whether of Militant or Bennite variety – was far weaker than its national profile allowed it to believe. There is no such pronounced and generalised shift to the right today, and all the movement in the Labour grass roots is to the left. Another is that the soft-Left was inordinately belligerent toward the hard-Left, and was happy to work with activists and politicians from the right in order to take control of the Labour Party. This profound realignment of forces, culminating in the victory of New Labour, was seen as a necessary modernising project, junking the unyielding dogmas of the past. Today, the soft-Left, having experienced the traumatic years of Blairism, is more likely to achieve some of its objectives with a left-wing leadership, and currently appears to be happy to live with such a leadership. And today's modernisers are in the Corbyn camp: 'socialism with an iPad', as John McDonnell put it.[87]

And for those not wearing the Cold War blinders, it is patently obvious that 'left-wing' means something far more cautious than it used to. Corbyn has sought to steer a careful course, compromising with the right-wing over NATO membership and the European Union. He has called for Labour councils to set legal budgets with deep spending cuts rather than defying the government. His shadow chancellor John McDonnell has dropped early plans for the nationalisation of energy firms, despite how popular such measures would be. There is also the difference made by the breakdown of the traditional media's ideological monopoly. Whereas the popular press in the early eighties was overwhelmingly right-wing, if not downright Thatcherite, the tabloids exert no such dominance today. However culpable and complicitous national media outlets may be, social media has broken their grip on the national conversation. And there is the very different role of trade unions in today's Labour politics. Whereas once, powerful right-wing union leaders could be relied on to battle their left-wing counterparts and give ballast to the red-hunters, there is little sign of even relatively right-wing union leaders signing up for sabotage.[88] Moreover, this time around there is no SDP to act as a right-wing pressure on the party, and there is little space for such a vehicle. Those looking for centrist politics with no trade union strings attached already have it in the Cameron–Osborne leadership. Finally, in the absence of the USSR, there is simply no groundswell of anti-socialist feeling which could be harnessed to a red-hunting crusade. Unilateral nuclear disarmament was once a policy nostrum associated with 'fellow travellers'. Today, the majority of the public, and much of the military establishment, favour scrapping it.[89]

None of this is to say that Corbyn's position is assured until the next election. The next chapter will deal with the considerable obstacles he faces. One might say that, even if he were to survive until the 2020 general election, and even if he were to win it, that is where his real problems would begin. However, those attempting to fight yesterday's battles in the hope of yielding yesterday's results, call to mind Anna Freud's famous saying that 'in our dreams, we can have our eggs cooked exactly how we want them, but we can't eat them'.

2
The Crisis of British Politics

Labour's Mess

In the BBC series, *The Thick of It*, hapless opposition leader Nicola Murray tries to win credit from a sceptical electorate by agreeing with a government policy. To appear tough, she decides to agree with a particularly mean-spirited austerity policy, cancelling funding for 'breakfast clubs' for primary school children. 'We are in concurrence with the government,' she intones, 'because we are in unity with the British people.' Just as she announces her support, however, the government backtracks. Her spin doctor, Malcolm Tucker, is furious: 'Nicola is about to adopt a policy that is so toxic that this stony-hearted government of fucking puppy killers is dropping it?'

Nothing else in popular culture captured so accurately the air of sheer pointless and self-defeating cravenness that has hung around Labour in recent years. Shadow Chancellor Ed Balls declaring, before a general election, that he would reverse none of the spending cuts that the government has introduced. Acting leader Harriet Harman, faced with a draconian welfare bill, whipping Labour MPs into the bold stance of abstaining. Unable to form a government, they couldn't form an opposition either. Labour had rarely looked this pitiful. And it is this Labour, ideologically vacuous, politically timid, unimaginative, that Jeremy Corbyn set out to change. In the event, this very weakness is what enabled Corbyn to win.

Corbyn's victory is evidence, then, not of the power of the Left but of the enervation of the Labour Party and of the traditional political centre. It would be a mistake for Corbyn's supporters to be too impressed by their own sudden feeling of vitality. It is equally a mistake for analysts to take too seriously the reports, red-faced and spittle-lathered, on the strength of Corbynism in the Labour Party. The new left-wing Labour group, Momentum, has attracted considerable support within the party, and recently won the Labour youth elections. Yet, that was on a turnout of 3.5 per cent.[1] The group, though talked up in the press the better to monster it, has as yet little clout in the real centres of power in the Labour Party. Constituency members are overwhelmingly supportive of Corbyn, but it would be too hasty to presume that they are all single-mindedly socialist.

On the same day that Corbyn won the Labour leadership, the old stalwart of the Labour Right Tom Watson won the deputy leadership. Diane Abbott was later defeated in the selection race for Labour's London mayoral candidate by the uninspiring Sadiq Khan, while the elections to the Conference Arrangements Committee that year were lost by the Left.[2] There are reasons why these candidates won apart from their politics. Watson is regarded as a decent politician who took on Murdoch and the child abuse scandals. Sadiq Khan is seen as having a certain personal charisma that Abbott lacks. But that is partly the point. Corbyn's supporters incline to the radical left, but they are by no means as experienced and programmatic in this as, say, the veterans of Eighties Leftism.

How, then, could a current so marginal within the Labour Party, so painfully at a loss for so many years, suddenly find itself swept to the leadership by a fusion of young, radicalised members and supporters with the existing networks of the hard-Left? Some of the answers to this question are contingent, and have to do with organisational changes to the Labour Party and tactical mis-steps on the part of its managing elites. Some have to do with the austerity politics which, until Corbyn's election, enjoyed bipartisan support in the House of Commons. However, the most important factor is also the most intractable – a secular crisis of the labour movement and its grass roots. As Ed Miliband put it in an important piece for the Fabian Society shortly after winning the leadership election: 'Five million votes were lost by Labour between 1997 and 2010, but four out of the five million didn't go to the Conservatives,' he wrote. 'One-third went to the Liberal Democrats, and most of the rest simply stopped voting. It wasn't, in the main, the most affluent, professional voters that deserted Labour either,' he continued. 'You really don't need to be a Bennite to believe that this represents a crisis of working-class representation for Labour – and our electability.'[3]

In this analysis, Miliband was undoubtedly influenced by the arguments of his close advisor Jon Trickett from Labour's soft Left.[4] However, for reasons I will outline in Chapter 2, Miliband was not able to reverse the losses. Labour's vote had crashed to its lowest level since 1918 in the 2010 election, and barely shifted in 2015. Labour's internal focus-group reports suggest that it may never win these voters back, as they have shifted to the right and are 'a hair's breadth from becoming Conservatives'.[5] It is an open question how representative such focus groups can be, and neither the British Election Study nor the Beckett Report into the party's defeat found much evidence for the idea that Labour wasn't right-wing enough for the voters.[6] However, where most analyses converge, it was on the idea that Labour lost first and foremost on the economy. The 'credit crunch' had destroyed its reputation in much the same way as 'Black Wednesday' had destroyed the reputation of the Conservatives. As it approached the election, Labour seemed able neither to defend its record nor to admit fault.

The decline was also felt in terms of party membership, which had fallen from over 400,000 in 1997 to 156,000 by the end of 2009. The fall was partially reversed in the first months of Miliband's leadership, rising to 194,000 by December 2010, but only during the Corbyn surge did it increase to anything like previous levels.[7] The official labour movement has been in a similar freefall, though over a much longer period, with trade union density falling from over 50 per cent in 1979 to just over a quarter in 2012. The fall has been pronounced in the public sector in recent years as austerity measures and recession have eroded employment, but the worst coverage continues to be in the private sector, where over 85 per cent of workplaces have never seen a union rep – and it is part of a global decline, registered first in the United States but apparent in all the core industrial economies.[8] In a weakened condition, unions had put up little resistance to austerity measures, barring a brief flurry of strike action against pension reforms in 2011, after which the rate of strike action fell to the lowest levels on record.[9] The labour movement, having become more top-down, more politically timid and more constrained by hostile legislation, has been poorly placed to put up much of a fight – in a way, supporting Corbyn's candidacy, as the big unions did, was by far the most radical thing they have yet done to address their existential decline.

As its institutions have become more top-heavy, and its social base weakened, the Labour Party has become more right-wing, more managerial and more dominated by middle-class professionals, hostile to the traditional aims of the Left. And just as it adjusted to the post-Thatcher consensus, so in recent years it embraced the austerian agenda of its opponents, offering only to temper its excesses – which, as Miliband discovered, was not enough to attract progressive voters to the polling booths. Instead, Labour ran the risk of what party activist James Doran called 'Pasokification', following in the doomed footsteps of its centre-left sister party in Greece as it administered austerity policies.[10]

Ironically, this very weakness, which left the Labour Party open to Corbyn's surge, is now one of the most significant

impediments to his success. And Corbyn's success as yet
has shown no tendency to reverse Labour's difficulties:
it may even compound them in the short-term. It is true
that throughout his campaign, hundreds of thousands of
people signed up as members or registered supporters of
the Labour Party. In the days following his success, further
tens of thousands joined Labour. The evidence now is that
these are sustained increases, and that the majority of the
new members remain supportive of Corbyn's attempt to
rebuild Labour from the left. Yet the fragility of this project
is visible in the abysmal poll ratings for Labour, which are
not even remotely strong enough among constituencies
that it needs to be winning over, particularly young people
and ethnic minorities.[11] Meanwhile, the constant barrage of
attacks on the Labour leader from a coterie of his own MPs,
echoed and amplified by a rabid media, ensures that whatever Corbyn attempts to achieve is repeatedly undermined
by a series of confected crises.

Democratic Decline

Labour is in trouble, then, but its problems are insepa-
rable from a wider democratic deadlock. In 2000, just as
the British electoral system was about to experience its
lowest participation rate in history, the political scientist
Colin Crouch coined the term 'post-democracy'.[12] From
the standpoint of post-Cold War triumphalism, such an
emphasis must perforce seem misplaced and unnecessarily
gloomy. At what time in history has democracy ever been
more globally institutionalised? In this strict and narrow

constitutional sense, within the framework of what could be called capitalist-democracy, the total number of people who could participate in elections to change their governments was probably greater at the turn of the millennium than it had ever been. So what was there to be gloomy about? The end of history had turned out alright, had it not?

Clearly, there is a great deal more to democracy than the formal existence of party-political competition and representative structures. Mass democracy has always depended upon popular engagement, and that engagement is undergoing a long decline. Parties and representative chambers are only as democratically robust as the power that is invested in them. If the locus of power shifts elsewhere, democratic capacity is lost. Further, for democratic institutions to be viable, they require a healthy degree of participation. Precisely what level of participation counts as healthy is a value judgement, but where there is a significant decline in voting turnout and party membership, there is a prima facie reason to begin asking questions. And this is exactly what we find. As Peter Mair puts it,

Party democracy, which would normally offer a point of connection and site of engagement for citizens and their political leaders, is being enfeebled, with the result that elections and the electoral process become little more than 'dignified' parts of the modern democratic constitution. That is, elections have less and less practical effect, because the working, or 'efficient' part of the constitution is steadily being relocated elsewhere.[13]

In the period between 1950 and 1990, there was a steady
state of trendless fluctuation in election turnouts across the
industrial democracies. After 1990, the average turnout
began to fall significantly, from 81.7 per cent in the previous
period, to 77.6 per cent in the 1990s, and 75.8 per cent in the
2000s. The trend was most advanced in the UK, where the
turnout in the 2001 general election was 'the lowest level of
turnout since the advent of mass democracy'. Most of the
record lows in turnout for other nations were recorded in
these two decades.[14]

In the British general election of 2010, average turnout
was 65.1 per cent, but the turnout varied across constituencies according to the social classes concentrated in those
areas, with a range between 44 per cent and 77 per cent.
Generally speaking, the more working class a constituency, the higher its rate of unemployment, the lower its
turnout.[15] Unsurprisingly given these trends, Labour has
been the biggest loser from declining turnout. Party membership has also slumped across European democracies. In
the 1960s, party membership as a proportion of the total
population averaged 14 per cent. In the 1990s, the proportion averaged 5 per cent.[16]

But there is another feature of modern democracies that
is relevant here, and that is the heightened electoral volatility of those who do still vote. If, as Mair argues, elections
no longer count as much as they did, then the likelihood of
strong party identifications declines, and choices become
more likely to be based on factors other than tribal filia-
tion. And, indeed, this is what one finds. Across European
democracies, without exception, one finds a marked decline

in strong party identification between the 1960s and the 1990s.[17]

What explains these trends? One way to approach this is to ask why it is that people are decreasingly inclined to participate in the system. Traditionally, abstention is viewed as a matter of 'apathy'. People decline to vote or join political parties, not from dissatisfaction, but from a sense of sufficient security and contentment in their consumer lifestyle that they have no motivation to vote. This was, in fact, the response of New Labour to a series of low electoral turnouts in 1998 – people stayed at home from contentment rather than disaffection. How well did this perspective explain the record low turnout in 2001? In part, the patterns of voting decline could be explained by the peculiarities of the electoral system. As Pippa Norris pointed out,

> Voting tumbled most sharply in safe Labour seats – places like Liverpool Wavertree, Stockport, Bootle – while falling far less in marginal Conservative seats such as Norfolk North and Hexham, where parties had greater motivation to mobilize support and voters had more incentive to feel that casting a ballot could make a difference to the outcome.[18]

But the broader picture was one of demoralisation and at most 'lukewarm support' for the government. One study found that for the first time the majority, some 62 per cent, of non-voters were deliberate abstainers – their non-vote counted as a rejection of the choice on offer. The same patterns are found repeatedly in subsequent elections with, one study suggests, all of non-voting in the 2005 general

election accounted for by deliberate abstention.[19] The
turnout never recovered to previous levels, and was never
higher than 65 per cent. In both 2001 and 2005, non-voters
constituted a larger share of the electorate than the vote
for the winning party. A local study of non-voters by the
University of York found that 80 per cent of those who
didn't vote in 2005 cited a lack of difference between the
major parties. As one respondent put it: 'Parties are all
brands nowadays. Brands of the same product.'[20] In 2015,
BBC News interviewed likely non-voters and found a per-
vasive sense of broken trust and cynicism: 'they're all the
same', and 'it won't make any difference', just two of the
more typical responses.[21]

The biggest non-voters are typically those who are most
likely to vote Labour: younger voters, poorer voters, and
those from ethnic minorities. In the 2010 general election,
only half of men aged 18–24 voted, while 39 per cent of
women from the same age range voted. Younger black and
Asian voters in particular began to peel away from Labour
in the 2005 general election, an election overshadowed by
the war in Iraq. And it is likely that while many of those
who did vote abandoned Labour for other parties such
as the Liberal Democrats or, in a few localities, Respect,
perhaps less than half of those voters actually turned out.
By 2015, only 33 per cent of black and Asian voters considered themselves certain to vote, compared to 52 per cent of
white voters.[22]

The evidence is overwhelming. There is a political withdrawal across the board, it is most pronounced among
those who were already least enfranchised, and the biggest

resultant losses in the UK have been sustained by the Labour Party. What accounts for this? If non-voters see themselves as being in protest against a system that seems unintelligible, distant and impervious to their concerns, what is the real basis for their alienation? To ask this is to ask something about what electoral participation is for. In the nineteenth century struggles over democracy, the concern of those who sought to prevent it was that it would lead to the erosion of the principle of private property. The reason that elites ultimately opted to extend the franchise to workers, however, was that they came to regard it as the easiest way of managing social disturbances. By committing, through a long and deliberately protracted process, to redistribute a proportion of wealth and power, they might avoid challenges to that power by other means. As Earl Grey, proposing the reforms, suggested: 'I am reforming to preserve, not to overthrow.'[23]

One way of characterising this state of affairs is to say that parliamentary democracy offers the possibility of some form of class compromise which ameliorates the conditions of those without property, while protecting the institution. In modern parlance, this is given a banal gloss in the form of Clinton's slogan on the key to electoral success: 'it's the economy, stupid'. Where there appears to be stable growth and employment, governments are popular, and political volatility is minimised. But this is to treat the economy as merely a technical factor in governing. In this view, the goal of efficient government would be to make investors as happy as possible, and watch the wealth and contentment pile up. But the economy is inherently political. It works, insofar as it does, through a tacit compromise between owners and wage-earners. Despite the hallelujahs and hosannahs for 'wealth creators' that politicians of centre-Right and centre-Left are inclined to engage in, businesses only bother to generate prosperity if the circumstances are acceptably profitable to them.[24] Employees, meanwhile, have to at least implicitly agree to the conditions that are necessary for profit-making. Stable governments are those which are able to secure a compromise between classes on the conditions of future growth.

In post-war Britain, it fell to a Labour government to begin the work of rebuilding a stable profit regime in which the state mediated between politically organised expressions of business and wage-earners. This class truce was accepted by the Conservative Party, which did little to undo it once in office. This was the high point of social democracy and, for approximately a quarter of a century, the peace held. Profits rose, but wages also rose in line with productivity, while a welfare state made up for the failures of the market with a social wage. For the duration of this period, electoral participation and party identifications remained strong, with turnout peaking in 1950 at 83.9 per cent, even if party membership showed a slight tendency to fall.

Following the deep-going crises of the seventies, the balance of the compromise was shifted such that organised labour was weakened, welfare was re-tooled as 'workfare' – a new disciplinary system to keep the unemployed on their toes – and the state took a growing interest in enhancing private sector profitability by reducing wage costs and removing regulations that businesses found obstructive, and opening up the public sector to commodification. These changes were legitimised by neoliberal ideology, and to some extent directed by those educated in it. Neoliberalism, broadly speaking, initially emerged as a break with classical liberal thought. Its pioneers were those like Ludwig von Mises and Friedrich von Hayek who, in the early twentieth century, regarded with horror the effects of mass democracy on the liberal order of private property. Regarding the emerging welfare state as a threat to property-based liberty, they initially looked to authoritarian Rightists to protect property, and then sought to reinvent the liberal state to protect it from democracy. According to their story, the essence of liberty was the ability to make choices with one's resources in a free market. Meanwhile, the essence of economic efficiency was unimpeded, quasi-Darwinian competition between rival producers, in which good ideas and practices would ineluctably out-compete the bad. Get the market out of the way and a pacific 'spontaneous order' would emerge which was far better for human welfare than government programmes. This, of course, was the soft sell. The slightly harder sell was General Pinochet. That is to say, this 'spontaneous order' had to be underwritten by a violently interventionist state, one whose repressive capacities were enlarged even as the democratic and welfare functions atrophied. Moreover, far from empowering 'markets', whatever this might mean, they tended to empower the largest, most economically powerful financial and industrial corporations on whose cooperation national governments depended.[25]

Perhaps one of the most sophisticated means of con-
straining democracy was the series of recommendations
endorsed by the 'public choice' school developed by
James Buchanan and William Niskanen.[26] Arguing that
state bureaucracies were necessarily inefficient and self-
serving, and that any 'public service' ethic was hypocrisy
writ large, they favoured the subordination of most public
functions to market-like mechanisms. Services should be
privatised or, if not actually run by corporations, should
emulate corporations where possible. Markets should be
introduced between providers, and competitive mechanisms set in place. Services should be removed from direct
political control where necessary: aside from full privatisation, the proliferation of quangos in British political life
was one of the early alternatives to democratic control.
This, of course, was anything but efficient. The companies
brought in to run services inflated costs drastically. Internal
markets notoriously inflated overhead costs in the NHS to
scandalous levels.[27] But what it did achieve was a crony
relationship between state actors and privileged businesses,
involving the state more deeply in making life easier for
business, while reducing its democratic capacities.

This internal reorganisation of the state was soon
accompanied by its integration into a network of international institutions – the World Trade Organization, the
European Union, and soon the Transatlantic Trade and
Investment Partnership – which collectively constrain governments in an 'iron cage' of regulations demanding fiscal
austerity, competition and privatisation in public services,
and the rolling back of laws deemed uncompetitive. The

scope for democratic participation grows narrower by the day. The net result is precisely what Crouch refers to as 'post-democracy':

> While elections still exist ... public electoral debate is a tightly controlled spectacle, managed by rival teams of professionals expert in the techniques of persuasion, and considering a small range of issues selected by those teams. The mass of citizens plays a passive, quiescent, even apathetic part, responding only to the signals given them. Behind this spectacle of the electoral game politics is really shaped in private by interaction between elected governments and elites which overwhelmingly represent business interests.[28]

In this view, it is not apathy that characterises a growing chunk of the electorate so much as their *exclusion* from effective political power. And matters are likely to get worse. One reason for this is that, since the credit crunch, the owners of capital are hoarding money rather than investing it.[29] This phenomenon is by no means restricted to Britain, yet in the UK alone, hundreds of billions of pounds are set aside rather than put to work to create jobs or growth. Profit rates being too low in the private sector, firms instead look to government to improve investment conditions by reducing the cost of labour and by creating new opportunities for them in the public sector: this is a far more important part of what the government calls 'austerity' than its spending cuts.[30] This exacerbates the peculiar and particularly corrupt form of relationship between the state and privileged sectors of business that is emblematic of the neoliberal era. But it also leaves Britain's economy weak, sluggish and ongoingly susceptible to crisis, and forces the state to be on hand, ever ready to lend new support and to extract more from a weary public. As the state becomes less and less democratic, and more geared toward crisis-management, the alienation and volatility of the electorate is likely to increase.

The other aspect of the popular withdrawal from parliamentary democracy that this brought about has been the withdrawal of governing elites 'into the institutions of the state'. As parties have lost their social roots, they have become more oriented toward 'office-seeking' in a way that is increasingly detached from their electoral success.[31] The extreme case of this is the technocratic coalition government wherein parties of whatever hue and social basis find themselves seeking to win a share of governing power in order to lead from the centre. Party leaderships are increasingly inclined to conceive of their power in terms of influence within the existing state apparatuses and non-elected institutions, assets which they can build up even as they lose electoral support.

A particularly crass example of this could be found in the run up to the 2015 general election, in which Nick Clegg (having won influence by securing the support of disaffected Labour voters anxious about the extent of planned austerity measures and increased tuition fees – subsequently to squander this support once in coalition) warned that a government without the Liberal Democrats would lack legitimacy.[32] Of course this proved to be untrue, but it suggested that Clegg's strategy for ongoing influence was not to win as many votes as possible – even then, the looming Liberal Democide was apparent to all – but to situate his party as parliamentary king-makers in exchange for some policy incentives and influence on select committees. But coalition governments of the centre are merely an extreme and unusually express example of what is generally taking place in a more granular, gradual and tacit way, visible in the growing profile of political professionals, special advisors, pollsters and focus groups whose existence increasingly appears to be about representing the government to the electorate, rather than the reverse. This partially explains why, given the choice between breaching an established governing consensus and cleaving to it while losing electoral support, party leaderships tend to choose the latter.

It is not that politicians are completely oblivious to their growing detachment and insulation from the public. Following the 2015 general election, Hansard described a 'deeply disillusioned citizenry that will be hard to motivate' to vote.[33] Later the same year, the House of Commons Liaison Committee began a series of hearings intended to address the decline of parliamentary institutions in British society.[34]

Its first report notes that, already in the late nineteenth and early twentieth centuries, the professionalisation of party machines, the strengthening grip of the executive of the state and the decline of parliament were already grounds for concern regarding the status of democracy in Britain. In its potted history, it also goes on to acknowledge the emergence of a stream of disengaged, 'antipolitical' sentiment rising in the Britain of the sixties, and the efforts made by some parliamentarians to reform an increasingly out-of-touch Westminster. Strange to relate, the closer its historical sketch gets to the present day, the wider the gap appears between the problem and the proposed solutions, which involved improving the functioning and powers of select committees. The political establishment knows that it is losing touch – it just doesn't have the smallest clue what to do about it.

'I read some Marx and I liked it': The Young Radicals Looking for a Political Home

It has been customary for some commentators, particularly those aligned to Labour, to bemoan the non-voting young as either huffy Kevin-the-Teenagers or Lauren Coopers, or as excessively discriminating to the point of self-indulgent. Polly Toynbee hits this particular sweet-spot of commentariat arrogance with a regularity that can't be accidental. Speaking of those who refuse to vote in defence of political principle – the majority of non-voters – she scolds,

> Their vote is far too precious to bestow on any of the parties on offer. No one is good enough for them, as if they expect a personal bespoke party, regardless of the necessary compromises in assembling a majority, blind to how parties work as portmanteaus of ideals and interests willing to travel together. Did those over-fastidious ones ever roll up their sleeves in the past five years to start a new party or movement, or shift an existing one?

Yet in the same breath, Toynbee complains about those who have rolled up their sleeves for anything other than the palest pink social democracy, above all those inclined to 'vote Green'. 'A vote', she stiffly rebukes, 'is not a personal accessory to show the world who you are.' Naturally, these very same commentators are those who have been most likely to complain about the mobilisation of the young behind Corbyn for 'ignoring the electorate'.[35]

Another way of looking at it is to suppose that those disproportionately young people who mobilised to support Corbyn have a longer perspective than the next election. That the ways in which they are, in fact, rolling up their sleeves to shift an existing party is a recognition that political change takes place on registers other than the parliamentary. That by trying to change Labour, they have reference to something more than the few hundred thousand voters in swing constituencies who typically decide election outcomes. What is at stake here is a generational change that, though it has been seen in other countries first, is now intersecting with Britain's democratic decline to produce this challenge to the status quo.

From the first ruptures of the anti-capitalist movement to Occupy; from Ecuador, Bolivia and Venezuela to Spain, Portugal and Greece, Leftist success has been propelled in large part by new movements of the young. Even in the United States, hardly a typical case in other respects, Bernie Sanders's support is overwhelmingly concentrated among the under thirties.[36] Much is written, not wholly incorrectly, of how these activists are shaped by 'post-materialist' values – support for peace and gay rights, for example. But far more fundamentally, this generation is the one to suffer the most from the consolidation of neoliberalism, as they are paying more for access to higher education, have far less access to diminished public services and welfare, and suffer far higher rates of unemployment. Their housing situation is, particularly in large urban areas, abysmal, and they are far less likely to have a chance of affordable rent, let alone home ownership. They face a more financially uncertain and later retirement than previous generations, as more of their old age income will be dependent on financial products. And they have inherited a political system that is less responsive and more insulated from public influence than since the universal franchise was first achieved. But if all that explains their militancy, it does not explain why it should now take the form of a highly improbable mass entry into Labour. What else could these activists be doing, if they were not trying to pull Labour to the left?

One of the major casualties of neoliberalism as it has been rolled out across Europe has been the classical social democratic party. Almost uniformly, albeit at different paces and to differing degrees, they found themselves overwhelmed by the transformations in the global economy and the resistance of business to their attempts to keep the old status quo going. As the priorities of national states switched from full employment, as a condition for the old class compromise, to counter-inflation and balanced budgets, as a condition for businesses to keep investing, social democracy abandoned the policy instruments that had made it distinctive. Only in Sweden and Austria was there a brief period in which counter-inflation existed successfully alongside extensive public sector investment and an institutional commitment to full employment, but this did not survive the turn of the nineties. In Britain, New Labour had consecrated neoliberal orthodoxy before its election in 1997, such that nothing else was expected. In France, a 'plural left' government led by the Socialist Party was elected just as the European Stability and Growth Pact was passed, committing all signatories to fiscal discipline. Although it was committed to a modest Keynesian programme, such as the thirty-five-hour week, it did not have to be coerced into respecting budgetary orthodoxy, keeping public investment under control and restraining wage demands. And in Germany, the Social Democratic Party was elected in 1998 with the Greens as coalition partners and with some idea of an interventionist state, but was already committed to fiscal orthodoxy and deep welfare cuts inspired by Clinton's move to 'end the welfare state as we know it'.[37]

In short, social democracy has lost its purpose in line with the loss of agency of parliamentary democracy to represent the electorate. In place of social democracy, a strange new hybrid form has emerged, sometimes called 'social-liberalism'. Although still functionally social democratic in the relationship to organised labour and the working-class electoral base, the leadership of such parties is undeniably neoliberal, and the direction of policy is aimed at gradually converting the base to a neoliberal common sense. This has proved costly in electoral terms, as this new breed of social-liberal parties have struggled to adequately distinguish themselves from their centre-right rivals. One result of this is that since 1989, a series of radical Left parties have emerged across Europe, to challenge the rightward shift of social democracy.[38] Pinning their hopes on a 'vacuum thesis', according to which the evacuation of a traditional social-democratic political space should leave space for a new Left, parties including the Rifondazione Comunista in Italy, the Front de gauche in France, and Die Linke in Germany, were launched to occupy the vacant space. Emphasising a modern combination of left-wing themes, from class politics to 'post-materialist' and left-libertarian concerns, they have fused old elements with the new: the remnants of traditional Communist Parties fused with defecting left-wing components of social democracy, a range of revolutionary fragments and activists schooled in the social movements and public assemblies.

Socially, these parties are far less supported by industrial workers than their equivalent older formations, the communist parties, and far more by the lower end of the salariat. Their support base also tends to be far more concentrated among those under thirty-five years old. These parties have thrived above all when they have remained aloof from coalitions with centre-left parties and maintained a policy of frontal criticism on markets, privatisation, redistribution and Europe, but their electoral success has been far in excess of their real social depth. These parties, it must be frankly admitted, have struggled to turn their electoral profile into real power. They have only in two cases, Spain and Greece, succeeded in fundamentally altering the dynamics of party competition. And in no case have they changed the neoliberal constitution of state power. Nevertheless, in terms of gaining some form of representation for a left-wing constituency that had been neglected, they have enjoyed some success.

So why did Britain not see an equivalent party form? It was not for want of trying: the ultimately abortive experiments in launching such ventures in the UK range from the Socialist Alliance, to Respect, to Left Unity. Only in the case of Respect were electorally significant results obtained, and even these were short-lived. These organisations proved to be far too narrow, based on ramshackle coalitions of the fragments of the far Left and the odd Labour refugee, to make a sustained bid for a national political presence. They gained minimal union backing and, in contrast to continental rivals, were not nourished by the addition of major splits from social democracy. Essentially, what prevented them from being more than protest parties was the demoralisation and defeat of the Labour Left.

The defeats that were inflicted on the British Left in the 1980s were, cumulatively, far more traumatic and disabling than anything comparable visited on their continental allies. From the miners to municipal socialism, every political and cultural organisation of the Left and the labour movement had defeats handed to them both by the Thatcher Government and by a Labour leadership determined to free itself to adapt to the new order. By the time Blair had taken control of Labour, their expectations were set to somewhere below zero. The broad lines of policy which they were compelled to accept were such that, however disappointed people may have been, there was no great galvanising shock when a New Labour Government began to implement policies previously associated with its electoral opponents, such as Private Finance Initiatives and market-based public sector reform. Only the prime minister's strange alliance with a right-wing US president in the prosecution of adventurist war produced a potentially life-threatening crisis for the Labour leadership, and even then only a single MP decamped – George Galloway, who was expelled rather than walking out of his own accord, much less leading any kind of split. Rather than split like other social-democratic parties, Labour simply haemhorraged members as well as voters.

Insofar as the young generation of radical activists have had a party orientation, therefore, it has taken the form of a weak identification with an alternative centre-left party such as the SNP, or the Greens. Otherwise, where they have been active it has tended to be in movements like Occupy, Radical Independence in Scotland, or single-issue campaigns such as Climate Camp. Corbyn emerged to articulate their discontents following several years of quiet demoralisation, as the UKIP Right held the initiative while the movements of 2010–11 went eerily quiet. As one Labour organiser put it, many activists had in the interim put down their copies of *The Coming Insurrection* and picked up the writings of Antonio Gramsci. They were thinking about how to build a movement as a 'system of alliances', as Gramsci had put it. One in which all who had lost out from the system, who were not represented in parliament, and whose voices were generally not heard in the media, would fuse into an effective political bloc.

Corbyn's advantage in this respect is his ability to personify the things that Britain's diverse progressive currents have in common, and to federate them. No other political format has as yet been up to the task. The Greens have assembled broad electoral support and increased their membership in recent years, largely by reducing the influence of its middle-class, right-leaning layers. However, precisely because of the existence of those layers and their record where it counts – for example, its management of Brighton council – it is distrusted by some on the Left. The SNP has succeeded in galvanising most left-of-centre voters in Scotland, but of course is limited by its strict national scope. Plaid Cymru, though it currently has a left-wing leadership, has thus far failed to make much impact on the left.

Corbyn's offer, in this context, was simple and unique. In joining the Labour Party or registering as supporters, they could bypass the need to patiently build an alternative party or start a new one. Instead, they could take the leadership in an existing mass party with union backing, money, and a record of electoral success far greater than any of its rivals, and drive it to the left. This did not mean turning Labour into a radical left party. It did not even mean giving Labour a radical left agenda. Corbyn's prospectus for a Labour Government may be one that only a hard-left leadership could secure today, but it is also one that would once have been advocated by the party's mainstream. Barring foreign policy, there is nothing in principle that Roy Hattersley couldn't support in Corbyn's agenda. It did mean pushing back against neoliberalism on several fronts, by rolling back privatisation, defending public investment, supporting welfare and placing local services back under local authority control. It did mean reversing Labour's usual foreign policy nationalism, and breaking with the previous bipartisan consensus on Trident.

What Corbyn's leadership did mean, for his supporters, was putting the Right on the defensive for once. It did mean turning Labour into a party where the radical Left could organise with resources and significant networks of activists. It did mean having some influence over policy, and beginning the task of opposing the austerity narrative in its fundamentals rather than some of its specifics. It did mean a once-in-a-lifetime chance to shift the balance of British politics to the left. Already, there is a new sense of optimism among activists who note that it was under Corbyn's far more oppositional leadership that government was forced to retreat on cuts to working families tax credits, and later on the government's unwholesome arms deal with the Saudi dictatorship. Labour had been running scared from opposing the government on key policies. Now Corbyn has demonstrated that opposition works.

The strategic problems looming for Labour's nascent new Left, however, are legion. First and foremost, since Labour is in the marrow of its soul a constitutionalist and electoral party, it is naturally built-in to the culture of the party to be obsessed with electoral outcomes to the near exclusion of other considerations. Already, Corbyn's most vitriolic backbench opponents are hoping for a drubbing in upcoming local elections, to expedite his overthrow. A defeat by 2020, which may be unavoidable whatever type of leadership Labour has, will undoubtedly be taken as a defeat for a socialist programme and the basis for a return to right-wing leadership. And yet, Labour was already in decline before Corbyn took the leadership. The sources of decline were deep and worsening over time, and will certainly not be reversed in Scotland, where the decisive damage was done during the independence referendum. If activists are to have any success in their longer-term objectives, they may have to be willing to at least tacitly accept that the short-term is going to be grim in electoral terms and that they are going to have to fight tooth and nail with the party establishment – who are far from innocent of Labour's current weakness – to prevent it from using these weaknesses to restore their dominance. There is no easy, cost-free route to changing the political consensus, much less building a robust left-wing organisation capable of doing so.

Second, as energising as the leadership victory undoubtedly was, and not disregarding the likelihood of left-wing gains at various levels of the organisation such as the NEC, Labour is still a party in which the power is overwhelmingly concentrated at the top. Like other parliamentary parties, it has become far more geared toward state administration even at the cost of its traditional representative functions. This is why thus far, Corbyn's need to reckon with the Labour backbenches, not to mention the dissenters in his cabinet, has arguably done more to shape his policies than the as yet unformed activist base. Quite how they are supposed to deal with this is not clear. Should they seek to deselect MPs who don't represent the membership? If they do, they run the risk of sharpening antagonisms well before they are able to win those battles. Should they attempt to reform the party's structures? Where to begin? If what they want is a genuinely democratic Labour Party, they will be trying to bring about something that has never before existed, and which goes against all the dominant tendencies in parliamentary democracies.

Third, what do they do with electoral victory? If Corbyn is, against all prevailing signals, able to win an election and tries to implement his agenda, that is when his problems will begin for real. There is no precedent in any of the core industrial democracies for success in reversing neoliberalism in this way. Greece is the only country in which a party has been elected to do this, and the result was that party's comprehensive humiliation, a form of waterboarding-by-negotiation at the hands of the Eurozone leaders and finance ministers, resulting in their accepting the agenda of their opponents and – even worse – selling it as victory. The result was utter demoralisation. What do Corbyn's supporters do if they find that the traditional prize of a Labour government is a poisoned chalice? Or, what do they do if they find that Labour is, for other reasons, no longer a hospitable place for them? How do they avoid being churned up in the party machinery or burned out in factional warfare? How do they ensure that they can come out on the other side with a chance of political survival? They would be unwise to get carried away by any illusions as to their current strength, as their opponents will exploit their overreach ruthlessly. They would be concomitantly wise to keep in mind just what kind of party they are trying to change, and the considerable odds against them. Labour, for all its genuine achievements and merits, may not be the kind of party they think it is. The next chapter explains why.

3

Labour Isn't Working: Whatever Happened to Social Democracy?

Labour's history as a parliamentary party is a story of failure far more often than it is a story of success. Labour politicians are certainly justified in boasting about the achievements of the Attlee administration, above all the welfare state, but how many can find anything to boast about in the interwar years, from the underachieving MacDonald-led administrations to the National Government which, to all intents and purposes, pioneered austerity and its 'we're all in it together' myth? Who looks back nostalgically on the Wilson/Callaghan era, from its lame ducks to its stagflation, or from devaluation to the social contract? The Blair/Brown administrations may have had no reforming ambitions to match those of previous eras, but few now think of its hallmark policies – Private Finance Initiatives, the Iraq invasion, low taxes for the rich, regulatory freedom for the bankers – as raving success stories. And not only is the story of Labour overwhelmingly one of failure. It is one wherein the conditions for any success once enjoyed have long since passed. The doctrinal coordinates which once underpinned social democracy everywhere – from the 'mixed economy' to welfarism, from public ownership to Keynesian intervention – will no longer avail, because global capitalism would reject these policy nostrums, much as a body rejects an organ implant.

So many of Corbyn's supporters – admittedly less so the younger variety – want 'real' Labour, 'old' Labour, 'traditional' Labour, what Labour is supposed to stand for. The allure of this idea is difficult to overstate. If there are risks in being too impressed by Corbynism, there is an equivalent danger in being transfixed by an idea of Labour that has never been close to reality. The only remedy for this is a cold, unsentimental look at what 'real' Labour might be (or have been), and why it might not be a satisfactory basis for what is to come. Rather than demonising New Labour as a cuckoo in the nest tearing up the fabric of social democracy, it would be useful to look at where the germs of Blairism were already present, and how they came to the fore. We should at least make space for the possibility that the problem, one way or another, is Labour.

If we are to understand anything about the prospects for Corbynism, we have to consider it as a moment in the degeneration of Labourism. It is the culmination of a series of defeats for a form of political organisation that seems to be inadequate in today's world. And it is probably headed for a defeat of its own. Such a setback, if it is not too demoralising, may ultimately permit the rethinking and regroupment that the Left desperately needs. But only if the nature of the beast is recognised early.

'The advanced wing of Liberalism'

The Labour Party always 'owed more to Methodism', asserts Tony Blair in a critique of Corbyn's leadership, 'than to Marxism'.[1] This shop-soiled cliché is solemnly incanted by Labour loyalists and pundits at every opportunity. If its purpose in Blair's case is to implausibly situate him as a legatee of Christian Socialism, its wider function is to stress the British exception. Labourism is held to have a unique status relative to European social democratic parties, most of which owed something to the Marxism of the Second International in their origins.

There are some elements of truth in the cliché. The Independent Labour Party's foundation in 1893 was accompanied by a Labour Church service attended by several thousand people, expressing the deeply religious, ethical element of the emerging ideology of labourism. Religious nonconformists certainly played a role in Britain's emerging trade union movement in the nineteenth century, and in the formation of Labour's moral ideology when it emerged. Keir Hardie was a Methodist, Ramsay MacDonald the product of a Calvinist sect, George Lansbury was a stalwart Anglican. The Labour Party, meanwhile, was unlike the German Social Democratic Party (SPD) in that while it had small Marxist currents, it had no party-wide affiliation to Marxism of any variety.[2] Yet, if all that is proven here is that religion had a role in forming the social life and ideological character of labourism, and that it did not pursue a Marxist agenda from its inception, this is not to say very much. What seems to have more enduring significance for the distinctive shape and trajectory of the Labour Party is its origins in Victorian Liberalism.

Before it was the basis of a political party, labourism was the near-spontaneous ideology of a dense network of labour movement organisations, from cooperatives to working men's clubs, gardening and brass band clubs to sports fans associations. In a difficult political environment shaped by the elimination of the Chartist movement after 1848 and the stabilisation of the British political system in the relatively affluent latter half of the nineteenth century, the labour movement had developed in the ruts and foxholes of working-class life.[3] It provided a defensive infrastructure in which workers could live and associate without having to challenge for political power. Politically, this tendency was dependent on the Liberal Party, from which a few mild reforms could be wrung very slowly, and which would even stand a few labour movement candidates known as 'Lib-Labs'. Intellectually, labourism was not exactly endowed with the most riveting champions – such a Leftist intelligentsia as existed in Britain at the time was either anaemically moralistic or redundantly schismatic. There was little to choose from between the sermons of the ethical socialists and the braying sectarianism of Henry Hyndman and his followers (only Britain could offer an ex-Tory, patrician product of Cambridge as its first leading Marxist intellectual).

When the franchise was achieved for a substantial number of male workers through the Second Reform Act of 1867, and later extended in a Third Reform Act in 1884, this was arguably more due to the stabilisation of British capitalism in the growth years after 1850 than it was due to persistent organisation on the part of workers. The political establishment was confident in its ability to extend the franchise while managing what Gladstone referred to as 'millions of hard hands'[4] who might otherwise pose a threat to the institution of private property.[5] And in the short-term, the parties of property had considerable success in ensuring that the votes of workers went into their own campaigns. It was a Tory administration led by Benjamin Disraeli which implemented the Second Reform Act, and Disraeli proved to be adept at winning workers to Conservatism on the basis of an appeal to empire and social reform. And if the majority of working class voters cast their votes for the Liberals, this was to little beneficial effect.

In frustration with the recalcitrant, obstructionist attitude of the Liberals, the Labour Representation Committee was founded in 1900 with the support of the Independent Labour Party, the Social Democratic Federation and the Fabians. The wider labour movement was, at this stage, in exceedingly poor repair. By 1888, only one in ten adult men belonged to trade unions. The Independent Labour Party, the precursor of Labour, had attained only ten thousand paid members by 1895, a number that had been cut in half by 1901. Trade unions had suffered a string of defeats, culminating in the damaging Taff Vale judgment of 1901, in which a court found that in common law, unions could be liable to employers for loss of profits incurred by strike action. Even within the Liberal Party, MPs representing organised labour represented only a small minority, amounting to only eleven by 1898, largely due to the obstruction of working-class candidates by constituency associations dominated by middle-class members.[6] The extension of the franchise had also proven to be severely limited, such that in the two general elections leading up to the First World War, only about 60 per cent of adult males were technically allowed to vote – the majority of those excluded being working class.

The purpose of the Labour Party, then, was not to conduct the militant energies of a rising working-class movement into the state. Rather, as it transpired, it was to more effectively lobby the Liberals, a refinement of the existing strategy. Ramsay McDonald had anticipated that 'the advanced wing of Liberalism' would be forced to 'sever itself from an old alliance and form itself into an independent Labour party'.[7] Having done so, the leadership of the new party declared their vehicle 'in the true line of the progressive apostolic succession from the Liberals'.[8] And in practice, as the Victorian era gave way to a more crisis-prone Edwardian regime, Labour proved to be vital in propping up Liberal dominance. Ross McKibbin writes that 'only with the support of the Labour Party and the Irish Nationalists' could the Liberals continue to govern at this point, the 'progressive alliance' being pivoted on the questions of free trade, which Labour defended, and the repeal of Taff Vale, which the Liberals were prepared to support.[9]

It was not until over a decade after the Labour Party was founded, with strike waves upsetting the political order from 1910 to 1914, that the labour movement came into its own. And there, the leadership came not from within the Labour Party – which abjured the strikes with displays of civilised horror – but from syndicalists whose focus was on the development of working class capacities for self-government outside the British state.[10] The indifference of these syndicalists to parliament could hardly be more at odds with the deferential attitude that most Labour politicians held toward the existing institutions of the British state, from the crown-in-parliament to the colonial empire. In fact, whatever else changed about the Labour Party in this era, one of its abiding attributes was to be the priority it accorded to the interests of the 'nation', and the deference it accorded to extant constitutional arrangements and military commitments. Those Labour MPs who, today, find simply unthinkable the break-up of the United Kingdom, the repudiation of Trident, and the end of the 'special relationship' with the United States, are in fact authentic legatees of their party's traditions.

But it was through the locust years of the Great War, largely supported by the Labour Party leadership – and by the majority of European socialist parliamentarians, with some notable dissenters – and the epochal rupture of the Russian Revolution, that the Labour Party was decisively formed as a national, centralised political party. Labour, despite its nominal commitment to opposing the coming of war, refuting the nationalist ideology that would justify it, and agitating for a general strike to obstruct it, was almost automatic in its support for the war once the British state decided to enter it.[11] Indeed, the fact of war instantly gave Labour an importance to Britain's ruling class it had hitherto lacked. Labour had always been in favour of a collaboration between classes to secure reform rather than outright class conflict, and its sociological basis in the trade union leadership arguably conferred on it a mediating character – negotiating between the demands of members and employers was the *raison d'etre* of a union bureaucrat. By becoming an active participant in the war effort, Labour in effect institutionalised this mediating role – so that it was no longer simply registering the demands of the labour movement in an electorally acceptable format, but also conveying the demands of the state to the labour movement in the interests of the war effort.

The party constitution devised in 1918 has been the source of a 'socialist myth' about Labourism. The call uttered in Clause IV for comprehensive public ownership and the recovery for workers of the fruits of their labour, much eulogised by Labour Leftists once the Blairites decided to overturn it, was never to be actualised in practice. The trade union leadership had accepted Clause IV to placate the Fabians and perhaps lend some ideological coherence to their own limited collectivist objectives, but they were only prepared to do so because it didn't make much difference to policymaking.[12] Indeed, the organisation of the party developed through this document was almost designed to ensure that the clause would not have to be realised. The sovereignty of the party conference was a piece of legal fiction, effectively guarded against by the block votes handed to the union leaderships who would tend to preserve a politically cautious orientation. At any rate, the binding force of conference was only to apply 'as far as may be practicable'. What emerged was an organisation that depended upon the mobilisation of socialists to achieve political power, but which ensured their sidelining in effective decision-making, the better to enable a potential governing elite to emerge. As Gregory Elliott acidly observes, 'The "iron law of oligarchy" announced by Robert Michels in *Political Parties* (1911) did not inexorably and imperceptibly assert itself in the post-war Labour Party. It was enacted at birth.'[13]

Nevertheless, here at last was a mass party of labour, fusing socialists and trade unionists, ready to displace the Liberals and become a party of government. The war had been, in one sense, a shattering blow to European socialism, elevating its nationalist and pro-colonial elements and marginalising its internationalists. The Russian Revolution had introduced a decisive cleavage in the socialist movement, as the left-wing of social democracy largely split to form communist parties. Yet, for Labour, the war had resolved a number of problems, allowing them to decisively break with the Liberals and allowing the leadership to reorganise itself as a potential governing stratum. It had also promoted trade unions to potential helpmeets of the state in its imperial capacities, since the industrial working class was essential to the state's ability to wage war on a modern scale.[14] Finally, with a distinctive mobilising ideology of social reform and public ownership, Labour was ready to take office.

From Zero to Less than Zero:
The First Labour Governments

The sociologist Frank Parkin, looking at the problem of working-class conservatism, suggested that an emphasis on conservatism as a puzzle to be explained was misleading. The real question, given the conservative nature of the dominant institutions – from the church to the military to parliament – was how anyone turned out to be a socialist.

Something similar can be said about the Labour Party. To the familiar Leftist complaint 'Why is Labour so conservative?' we might respond, 'How could we expect them to be anything else?' It is futile to speak of 'betrayal'; this is nothing more than the distress call of the disappointed utopian. Indeed, given Labour's fundamental strategic orientations, its institutional context, and the nature of the system that it seeks to manage, nothing is so utopian as to expect this party to bring about radical transformation. The exception of the Attlee administration is hardly negligible, but that highly unusual moment is not given its due, hardly taken seriously enough at all, unless it is contrasted with Labour's broader record in office.

By the turn of the twenties Labour had converted itself into a party of administration, its leadership integrated into the state and ready to govern. Yet the party of labour, on the brink of taking office, had still not proven to actually *be* a party of labour. In fact, Labour's command of the working-class vote continued to be severely limited. By 1922, with just short of 30 per cent of the vote, it had 'failed to break through' in Birmingham, Liverpool, Bristol, Hull and

Cardiff, and won only nine seats in London. It was a party of urban workers in mining and certain textile areas.[15] The failure to hegemonise even the industrial working-class vote, let alone the votes of rural workers or the middle class, led Labour to moderate its appeal, and stress its long-standing 'national', inter-class thematics.

So it was that in 1923, when Labour finally achieved enough seats to form a minority government with Liberal support, MacDonald reassured both the King and the wider public that Labour would 'not be influenced ... by any consideration other than national well-being'.[16] This had both domestic and colonial aspects. As colonial minister, former railway union leader J H Thomas offered assurances that he was there 'to see there is no mucking about with the British Empire', and duly proved his mettle in this regard by sending RAF bombers to Iraq.[17] On the home agenda, MacDonald's ministry kept its sights low, noting that a minority government could not be expected to achieve all that much. Such nugatory reforms as it did offer included improvements to housing and welfare provision, and some tax cuts paid for by a budget surplus – including cutting taxes on corporate profits. Given the scale of the problems a Labour government might have been expected to address, such as mass unemployment and deprivation, the rich would have had every reason to expect an attack on their class privileges. Chancellor Philip Snowden, however, was pleased to note that his budget was received warmly by the rich 'who had feared that there might be drastic impositions on their class'.[18] Indeed, Labour ministers seemed to enjoy greatly their chance to mingle with those whom

MacDonald called 'kings and rulers of the earth', on 'terms of equality'.[19]

This first, exceptionally brief, spell in office ended after just over nine months in the squalid scandal of the 'Zinoviev Letter', a forgery sent to the Foreign Office and the *Daily Mail* purporting to describe a Bolshevik policy of subversion in Britain. Labour, already under pressure from the Liberals and Conservatives over their supposed softness on Bolshevism, supported publication of the document – but this, and their consistent opposition to Communism, did nothing to lessen the attacks of their rivals. The chief result of this was not to damage Labour's electoral standing – indeed, while losing seats, it increased its share of the vote – but to finally finish off the Liberals by frightening their anti-socialist voters into the camp of the Conservatives.

Nothing illustrates Labour's parliamentary dilemmas in this era more than the bitter general strike of 1926. The issue at stake was that the coal owners were determined to reduce wages and, while not agreeing to the full extent of the cuts, the Conservative Government was determined to assist them in doing so – even if it meant, as their own Commission suggested, reducing living standards to pre-war levels. To this end, extensive preparations had been made on the government's side to ensure that coal supplies would continue in the event of a strike, while rhetoric against trade unions and 'Bolshevism' was ramped up. And while the union membership became more militant in the face of this, the General Council of the TUC panicked at the idea of such a giant confrontation. J H Thomas, acting as the TUC's chief negotiator, 'begged and pleaded' for some form of compromise from the government – 'give us some terms never mind what they are, no matter how bad they are'. But the Baldwin administration, well-prepared and in a bullish mood, insisted that the looming strike threatened 'the basis of ordered government'. 'It is not wages that are imperiled,' Baldwin charged, 'it is the freedom of our very Constitution.' MacDonald, though he had pledged to fight the corner of the miners from within parliament, assured the benches that 'with the discussion of general strikes and Bolshevism and all that kind of thing, I have nothing to do at all'.

The Labour leadership thus saw the strike as 'an unmitigated disaster, threatening Labour's claim to be a constitutional party'. The strike, the largest in British history, was adroitly encircled and dismantled by a government having wide recourse to emergency measures, police and military crackdowns and a stentorian campaign of vilification. The Labour leadership may have been reluctant to support outright class warfare; the Conservative government, though invoking the language of the nation, was not. Nor was it above using subsequent legislation, the Trade Disputes Act of 1927, to attack Labour's political levy. These developments, in toto, 'helped to accelerate Labour's rightward drift'.[20]

The Labour minority government that was elected in 1929 was in a much stronger position than the last. It finally had more seats than the Conservatives, and enjoyed the support of a Liberal Party that had radicalised around an agenda of reflationary measures and state intervention. It therefore had more chance of achieving some of its goals than ever.

But, what were Labour's goals? Any hope that a Labour government would usher in radical change were squashed given Ramsay MacDonald's conventional cabinet, which comprised 'a familiar mix of moderate politician-trade unionists ... middle-class former Liberals ... intellectuals ... and "mild" ILPers'.[21] Only the appointment of George Lansbury, the left-wing former mayor of Poplar who had led a local rebellion against the payment of rates, edited the socialist *Daily Herald*, and was staunchly pacifist, could be seen as in any sense unconventional. The appointment of the economically orthodox Philip Snowden as chancellor, meanwhile, was the clearest possible signal that the new government would do little to tackle what it identified as its greatest issue, the problem of unemployment. Even before the October stock market crash, Labour had campaigned on this under the slogan, 'The Works Are Closed, But The Ballot Box Is Open.' Yet Labour had few specific policies to deal with it, and the absence of any serious strategy became clearer as capitalism began to enter its worst crisis yet.

This is not to say that the government lacked options. Oswald Mosley, then a Labour minister, proposed a 'Memorandum' endorsing measures to protect industries and support demand through the expansion of credit, increases in pensions and other allowances. There was also the option of a coalition with the Liberals on the basis of their stimulus proposals. The party leadership, desperate for respectability, struggled to form a cross-party consensus, appointing a council of intellectuals, businessmen and trade unionists to hammer out a policy. In the end, chancellor Snowden persuaded the party to endorse the Treasury's orthodoxy that the only responsible economic policy was to allow markets to operate more or less unimpeded.[22]

As was often to be the case in Labour's history, the abstract commitment to 'socialism' was invoked to justify this retreat. In principle, Labour would bring about the supersession of capitalism by winning a 'socialist majority' in parliament and then securing gradual social reform and transitional measures within the context of buoyant capitalist growth. Any policy with an object less far-reaching than said transformation – say, the defence of workers' living standards during recession – could be, where convenient, denounced as mere tinkering. This meant that capitalism had to be allowed to succeed one way or another. Given the cabinet's lack of confidence in any alternative growth formula, and its deference to the Treasury, this meant letting the City of London rule. Parliament, Chancellor Philip Snowden told the Labour Party conference, should not intervene in the financial matters of the nation, since 'Parliament is not a competent body to deal with such highly delicate and intricate matters.' Instead, as Treasury receipts tumbled, Snowden demanded 'drastic and disagreeable measures' to cut public spending.[23] This early austerity project was justified by a familiar 'all in it together' sentiment, but most of the required 'savings' were found in unemployment insurance.

In order to implement these cuts more effectively, MacDonald tendered the resignation of the cabinet and entered into a 'National' government in coalition with the Conservatives and Liberals. The new administration immediately implemented stringent austerity measures, balancing the budget and thereby 'restoring confidence' – that, inevitably, of investors. Having implemented this policy, the government dissolved itself and called a general election. The 1931 general election destroyed all participants in this coalition except for the Tories, who gained an unprecedented 55 per cent of the vote. The Liberals broke up into three factions for the election, whose total vote was barely above 10 per cent. And Ramsay MacDonald's faction, standing as 'National Labour', polled a mere 1.5 per cent. In the wider arc of history, it is clear that the Tories had been on a long upward electoral curve since the late 1800s, a trend that peaked in the 1930s. Baldwin, one of the more astute Conservative leaders, had understood the elements of this shift well; although a growing layer of British society had been moving to the left since the turn of the century, much of the remainder was available to be corralled into an anti-socialist electoral bloc led by the most combative defenders of private property. As such, the subtlety of the Conservatives in this period had been to allow just so much reform – be it pensions or the extension of the franchise to female voters – as would take the edge off any radicalising tendencies, while also banging the anti-communist drum louder than anyone else. Despite the Conservatives' political dominance of the inter-war period, for example, there is some evidence that the growing welfare consensus which Baldwin felt compelled to accept was having some mildly redistributive effects.[24] The Liberals, torn between Victorian nostrums of 'free trade' and fiscal abstinence on the one hand, and a 'new liberalism' enjoining welfarism and state intervention on the other, were unable to lead this bloc, and their period in 'National' government was just as fatal, in its way, as the more recent rose garden nuptials between David Cameron and Nick Clegg. The electoral system produced a clear division between a savvy Conservative Party, and a Labour Party that was as yet electorally underdeveloped, strategically vapid and tactically timid.

In coalescing with the Conservatives on an austerity platform, MacDonald's wing of the Labour leadership believed that – against the 'sectional' purposes of trade unionists but consistent with their particular ethical socialist tradition – they were putting 'nation' above 'class', something their critics decried as class treachery. However, the pall of MacDonald's ostensible 'betrayal' may obscure something important here: as if, by putting the problem in moral terms, we can sidestep the strategic problems raised, not just by parliamentary socialism, but even by the limited goal of welfare capitalism in an era of economic depression.

Those of us living through the era of many 'grand coalitions' between social democratic and conservative parties, often in the interests of implementing spending cuts (Greece 2011, Ireland 2011 and 2016, Italy 2013, though not Spain 2016), are in an advantageous position to understand this. Social democratic parties that have funded their welfare commitments on the basis of booming capitalism, or in some cases on the basis of *future* growth (the Greek state's borrowing in the boom years being a case in point), have found themselves compelled in leaner years to pursue austerity policies identical to those of their traditional electoral rivals – even at the cost of losing their electoral base and becoming a mere caste of state managers. The rise of radical left parties, from Syriza to Podemos, is at least in part a result of this realignment of social democracy to the neoliberal centre.

For the managers of social democracy, the attempt to resist these cutbacks and gross transfers of wealth to the private sector was hopelessly utopian. Even if they felt the depth and speed of austerity driven by Angela Merkel and conservative technocrats was too severe, there was no working alternative model of growth on the horizon. And even if the private sector was sluggish and investment pitifully low, there was no question of any other sector leading a new round of growth. Certainly, any government which involved the state in taking over the means of investment and attempting to create new growth through public works would face the risk of stiff resistance from business, banks, civil servants, media, and of course European institutions. The legality and constitutionality of their actions could be challenged, and they might face continual crises and challenges from within. They would risk even lower rates of investment, downgrading by the ratings agencies such that borrowing would become impossible, and speculative attacks. It should not be so surprising, therefore, if we repeatedly find social democratic leaders, egged on by establishment media, capitulating to the agenda of their opponents with an air of heroic self-sacrifice.

So, if the second Labour government in British history had ended once again in a debacle from which the Conservatives were the primary beneficiaries, it is rather too convenient to castigate the renegacy of a few short-sighted or corrupt leaders. It is neither an aberration nor an accident that Labour, from being the 'advanced wing of liberalism', became the rearguard of reaction: their means could have no other yield. Nor did the Labour Party, freed from such renegades, demonstrate renewed efficacy in opposition. The election as leader of Lansbury, a figure comparable in many ways to Jeremy Corbyn, confirmed a turn to the left in the trade unions and party grass roots. But his period in charge lasted only three years, in large part because his pacifism and commitment to disarmament brought him into conflict with the party establishment. Under neither Lansbury nor his successor, Clement Attlee – a monarchist from the party's Right – did Labour play a significant role in organising or supporting the rebellions of the unemployed. The Jarrow March has entered into labour movement legend, and it is for this reason generally forgotten that the Attlee leadership disowned the protest. And while much of the criticism of Lansbury's pacifism was justified by the need to defend Europe against fascism, Labour cheerfully supported the mendacious policy of 'non-intervention' in Spain, where the democracies quietly endorsed extensive fascist intervention on Franco's side. Labour in the 1930s did little either to defend its constituencies, to slow the advance of fascism or, concomitantly, the drift to war: and deviated not one iota from the narrow electoral path upon which its strategic purview had always been staked.

In truth, this was not just a problem with the Labour Party. Social democrats of various ideological hues and pallors had entered governments across Europe in the interwar period, and the record was with few exceptions abysmal. For example, as Adam Przeworski writes of this period, despite their ideological commitments to redistribution of wealth and socialisation of the economy, the riches of the upper classes were left largely untouched and not a single industry – barring the French arms manufacturers – was nationalised in this period.[25]

Labour in the 'Golden Age'

How, then, was the Attlee government of 1945–51 so different? For the first time in its history, Labour had won a landslide with almost half of the total vote, and a parliamentary majority of 145 seats. Its manifesto committed it to policies far more radical and far-reaching than any previous Labour electoral programme: a cradle-to-grave welfare state, a national health service, Keynesian economic intervention, extensive public ownership, mass house-building and much more. What is more, its actual accomplishments in these respects – even setting aside the mythopoeic eulogies – can hardly be disdained as trivial. The reformist road to socialism had twice led, in the interwar period, to a sad diminuendo of hopes and a shift to the right. Now, Labour instituted a series of stunning, seemingly irreversible reforms that transferred some of the country's wealth to workers in the form of an expansive social wage. Why?

It is commonly assumed that the war years had accelerated a long-brewing radicalisation in the British public, producing broad popular support for Labour's agenda. Here, surely, was the long-awaited vindication of the

Labourist strategy: popular support for socialism had reached the decisive tipping point, and Attlee's team had only to present their agenda for it to receive broad popular endorsement; and only to win a plurality in order to see those plans realised. Certainly, after the resignation of the pro-appeasement Neville Chamberlain in 1940, there was an overwhelming mood against Conservatism which – given the prevailing electoral winds – would tend to favour a Labour government. This was concurrent with a broad, nebulous 'antipolitical' sentiment aimed at the old governing elites, and support for some substantial reforms.[26] Tory opposition to proposed welfare reforms recommended in a 1942 report by the Liberal economist Lord Beveridge compounded the emerging mood against them. Yet, even if Labour's manifesto declared the party to be 'socialist, and proud of it', it would be exaggerating to call this a 'socialist' consensus. And few anticipated at the time that it would result in a Labour government – sources on both left and right expected a comfortable Conservative majority headed by a popular wartime prime minister who was not personally tarnished by the policy of appeasement.

Just as important as popular disaffection with the Tories was the confidence that Labour had in its reform agenda. Here, Labour gained vital experience from its participation in the wartime coalition government, which used Keynesian stimulus and demand-management techniques to keep production at a pace necessary for the successful prosecution of the war. This shift in statecraft was driven, in part, by the more far-sighted elements of the civil service, who placed liberal reformers in key state apparatuses.[27] The scarcity of labour during the war had raised the political power and bargaining leverage of organised labour, and encouraged the government to use collective bargaining to manage ongoing struggles over wages.[28] In addition, the precarious state of British capitalism, like that of many of its European competitors, was such that a radical government had a unique window of opportunity to reform the system before the usual business opponents of such reforms had a chance to become sufficiently organised. It is arguable that many of these changes would have been imposed upon a Conservative administration, and something like this is suggested by the record of centre-right governments across Europe in this era. Certainly, once they were in place, the Tories evinced no appetite for rolling them back, despite a brief, testerical campaign against 'socialism' in the elections of 1950 and 1951. No doubt this was in part because, despite exploiting real popular discontent with rationing and linking such policies to 'socialism', the Conservatives only gained office in 1951 due to the irregularities of the first-past-the-post system. Labour had in fact won slightly more votes than the Conservatives, and the Tories' polling suggested to them that they needed to accept existing social democratic policies if they were to win support among skilled workers.[29] As such, the Conservatives held on to governmental power, once obtained, by preserving rather than rolling back Labour's reforms. However, whereas Labour took advantage of its strength to implement sweeping reforms, the Conservatives would have resisted them as far as possible, and it is difficult to believe that anything like the National Health Service could have emerged from a government led by Winston Churchill.

However, if we are not to buy into maudlin myth, it is also necessary to place these changes in a broader perspective. Labour, having equated the socialisation of industry with public ownership, nationalised important industries such as steel, coal, railways, cars, telecommunications and the Bank of England. A full fifth of industry was taken into public ownership. But most of these firms were incapable of surviving alone at any rate, and their sustenance was necessary for renewed capitalist development. The owners of the firms were generously compensated with public funds and borrowing, so that they could reinvest in the profitable parts of the private sector. Meanwhile, the public corporations were preserved on the model of private industry, with the usual worker–management hierarchies, and their production decisions made on the basis of what was good for private business – their management often drawn from the capitalist class. Once stabilised, the system also proved remarkably resistant to further such encroachments on private ownership.

At any rate, the architects of the nationalisation programme, such as Herbert Morrison, were reluctant to extend it, arguing that Labour had to 'consolidate' its gains before attempting further transformation. Even the Labour Left began to retreat and soften its positions, partially in view of the growing anti-communist climate of the Cold War. Later, post-war social democrats of the Labour Right, such as Anthony Crosland and Hugh Gaitskell, argued that with a 'mixed economy' and some degree of political liberalism,

Labour had actually achieved socialism. Capitalism, if not in fact done away with, was grievously weakened by the encroachments on its power by organised labour and the social-democratic state. Since the Tories pledged to maintain the status quo, there remained only the consensus of 'Butskellism' (named after the Tory and Labour chancellors, Rab Butler and Hugh Gaitskell) to administer.[30] In some respects, Labour became a prisoner of its own exaggerations, contributing to an intellectual consensus – obviously bearing little relation to reality – that Britain's wealth was being so radically redistributed as to ultimately lead to what Lionel Robbins bemoaned as 'propertyless uniformity'.[31] One would hardly know, in the face of such fantastical assertions, that by the sixties, still some 75 per cent of personal property was owned by the top 5 per cent of the population.[32] Even absent such extravagant claims, the tendency was to treat Britain as an 'affluent society' in which major social problems had been more or less solved and poverty had largely disappeared. Such was the mood music to a long period of Tory dominance – as Macmillan argued, 'You've never had it so good.'

There is also an unsavoury side to the Attlee administration, inasmuch as such reforms as were achieved were coterminous with financial orthodoxy, the continuation of rationing alongside increased exports, a willingness to use troops to break strikes, and wage freezes. A forgotten aspect of the 'golden age' is indeed this pungently authoritarian side of Labour administrations. Labour was in some respects more avid than the Conservatives in prosecuting the war against organised labour and, later, social movements. Attlee's government repeatedly deployed armed forces against striking workers, invoking wartime anti-strike legislation. Later, it was the Wilson administration of 1964–70 which first deployed the notorious Special Patrol Group in London, while developing legislation to severely curtail the unions' right to strike. In the crisis-ridden 1974–79 Wilson–Callaghan era, Barbara Castle did not hesitate to use armed forces against striking firefighters. Even the famously liberal Home Secretary Roy Jenkins tilted the balance of criminal justice policy in an authoritarian direction with his contribution to Britain's repertoire of 'anti-terrorism' laws, the 1974 Prevention of Terrorism Act authorising internment and jury-less trials in Northern Ireland, while the Criminal Law Act introduced further restrictions on organised labour.[33] The authoritarianism of New Labour was of a different order, but hardly unthinkable in light of the record of social democracy in its heyday.

The post-war consensus was also bought in part with American dollars, which ensured Britain's orientation in a new axis of power which demanded continuity in foreign policy justified by a staunch anti-communist line. Despite manifesto commitments and pre-election insinuations, Labour's Ernest Bevin had promised on election day, 1945, that the new government's foreign policy would not differ from the previous one. His first parliamentary speech as foreign minister made clear that he accepted the policy of his Conservative predecessor, Anthony Eden.[34] He did not dissimulate. Labour had, in 1944, supported the policy of crushing the Greek partisans and supporting monarchist forces. And while it orchestrated the British withdrawal from India, it offered no such relief to Kenya or Malaysia, where brutal counterinsurgency was indicated.[35] Similarly, it would go on to send troops to assist the French restoration in Vietnam, support Nato (despite noisy opposition from the Left), and develop nuclear weapons. Here, then, was the zenith of social democracy: Labour had achieved as much as it was ever likely to, finally establishing the long sought after compromise between the classes, and its commitment to 'nation' never wobbled.

The crucial delusion, common to Labour leaders of the era, was that a new economic formula had been reached for unprecedented, perpetual expansion, which would support an ongoing class compromise. As Stuart Hall wrote in a critical review of the post-war system, they believed that 'the social democratic bandwagon could be hitched to the star of a reformed capitalism: and that the latter would prove capable of infinite expansion so that all the political constituencies could be "paid off" at once: the TUC and the CBI, labour and capital, public housing and the private landlord, the miners and the Bank of England'.[36] To this effect, it is sometimes assumed that the economic controls implemented by Labour were Keynesian in drift. In fact, although the term 'Keynesian' may at times be a convenient marker for the kind of economic controls used in the post-war period, the counter-cyclical measures implemented by post-war Labour governments tended to involve 'taking the economy off the boil' rather than reflationary measures in the down-swing.[37]

The post-war boom had arguably little to do with a uniquely Keynesian policy mix and much more to do with the space for new investment created by the catastrophic destruction of capital during the war. And insofar as the new consensus depended on an unusual period of capitalist dynamism, with close to zero unemployment and growth rates stabilising at 3 or 4 per cent, the first green shoots of capitalist failure were destined to vitiate that consensus. Of course, it was precisely the condition of unprecedented economic growth underpinning Labour's class compromise which began to absent itself toward the late 1960s – catching the Labour Government, then with a solid majority, totally unprepared.

The Collapse of the Consensus

The seeds of downfall were already partially visible when Harold Wilson, then something of a 'bright young thing' by Westminster standards, led Labour to victory in the 1964 election. Most signals were optimistic. Wilson, though he was from the centre, was reviled by the Gaitskellites and able to garner the support of the Left. Thanks to left-wing support, he was able to take the leadership after Gaitskell's death in 1963. He was careful to avoid outright attacks on 'fellow travellers' in the fashion of his predecessor, and evinced an informality and comic turn that went with the grain of popular culture. Labour under his leadership was elected to government on an ambitious project for full employment and public investment, breaking thirteen years of uninterrupted Conservative rule.

At first, everything seemed to be going exceptionally well, despite the tiny parliamentary majority with which

the government was formed. Labour began to implement
its National Plan for industry, secured agreement with
the CBI and TUC, and implemented many of its policies
including pension increases, rent controls and the abolition
of prescription charges. This may not have been the sweeping transformation of 1945, but with the Tory opposition
scattered and in decline, there was reason to be optimistic. Further, despite the enduring influence of Gaitskellite
revisionism and the talk of 'affluence', the limits of the post-
1945 settlement were becoming visible – the existence of a
wide swathe of impoverished people, especially pensioners,
was recognised.[38] Even the early attempts by Lord Cromer,
the Governor of the Bank of England and a close ally of the
City, to force a reverse in policy were seen off. Speculative
attacks on the currency – which Cromer advised Wilson
signified investors' demands that the government row back
from its policy of full employment, use incomes policy to
stifle wages and raise interest rates – were not enough to
force the government's capitulation at this stage. In the
end, Cromer was replaced and returned to the family mer-
chant bank Barings. Labour was confident enough in 1966
to call a new election and extend its mandate, gaining some
48 per cent of the vote compared to the Tories 41.4 per cent.
And despite the enduring influence of revisionism, this was
clearly a class vote: despite the fact that the Labour leadership was predominantly middle class, it scored the highest
share of manufacturing workers' votes in its history, some
69 per cent.[39]

How, then, did the government end up implementing
the bankers' desiderata? The underlying problem for the

government was that Britain was a declining global power, notwithstanding the efforts – largely supported by Labour – to preserve as much as possible of the colonial empire. As exports fell, Britain was faced with a balance of payments crisis, resulting in further speculative attacks and a choice between currency devaluation and import controls. The Treasury's policy had always been that the currency should be defended at all costs, and Wilson certainly agreed that a strong pound was central to Britain's global dominance. So while Wilson didn't cave in to Cromer's pressure, Labour was certainly determined not to alienate the City. Even the earliest budgets, which did pass some radical measures, tended to be deflationary in effect. Wilson's cabinet therefore overwhelmingly opted for a policy of import controls and deflationary measures to manage the crisis. They did not know, however, that Wilson had negotiated a deal with the Johnson administration in which, for a bail-out of the pound, Britain pledged to deflate the economy and use an incomes policy to restrict wages, while at the same time preserving its East of Suez military commitments and backing the United States in its war in Vietnam. Then, as now, Britain's global role was secured by latching onto the coat-tails of the White House. The National Plan was in effect dead by July 1966, as the government implemented a mandatory wage freeze across the board, the first since 1931, and cut public spending. The wage freeze necessitated one of the government's first fights with organised labour, as seafarers went on strike for a modest pay-rise which, the government claimed, would 'breach the dykes of the incomes policy'.[40]

Finally, in 1967, with the speculative attacks continuing, the government agreed to devalue the pound. The government quickly lost credibility, both among workers who resented growing unemployment and wage restraint, and among the affluent middle classes for whom the episode demolished Labour's economic credibility. The IMF were brought in to manage this process, and it was they who argued for the introduction of prescription charges among other things: a reversal that was implemented, with great embarrassment, in 1968. Dick Crossman asked the Chancellor Jim Callaghan at the time if he might increase family allowances for the poor: 'sorry, old boy, the IMF won't allow it'. Unto which: 'so we're back under the control of the bankers'.[41]

This was not just a case of government going awry. Certainly, Wilson could have devalued earlier and avoided some of the consequences of this protracted dance-off with the speculators. But the forces eating away at Labourism went deeper. The sixties had seen the emergence of two trends that would erode the Labour coalition. The first was the emergence of immigration as a major political issue after the 1962 Commonwealth Immigrants Act which, by enacting the first major restrictions on migration to the United Kingdom from the former colonies, exacerbated a simmering racist anti-immigrant backlash that was effectively harnessed by the Tory Right. The greatest successes for this strategy were enjoyed by the Tories in the West Midlands, where Labour had struggled most to rebuild its vote after a long period of Tory dominance amid relative regional prosperity. There, the right-wing in alliance with local press generated local panics about the arriving migrant populations. By winning the Smethwick seat in the 1964 general election on the slogan, 'If you want a nigger for a neighbour, vote Labour,' the Conservatives found that it was possible to gain working-class support without offering the usual class incentives. Indeed, Enoch Powell acted as a pathfinder for a New Right built on this discovery, that one could build a popular, right-wing coalition as long as racism was at the centre of it.[42] The second development was the growth of Welsh and Scottish nationalisms, coupled with civil strife in Northern Ireland, where the Catholic population was organising against Britain's own miniature version of Jim Crow. The gradual cession of the empire was raising questions about the purpose of the United Kingdom, while Westminster's antiquated institutions alienated growing layers of the middle class in Scotland and Wales. Labour lost its Carmarthen seat to the Welsh nationalists in 1966, then lost its Hamilton seat to the Scottish nationalists in the following year. In 1969, the paramilitary wing of the Ulster constabulary was deployed against Catholic protesters, with bloody consequences.

By the time Labour had lost the 1970 election, the British state to which the party had always deferred was in need of major renovation, while the post-war social-democratic coalition was falling apart. Some voters simply abstained, reflected in a turnout of 72 per cent, the lowest since the war, while others – including many manufacturing workers – decamped to the Tories. Worse than electoral losses, however, was the fact that the economic basis for post-war social democracy was disappearing, and Labour had few means by which to adapt to new circumstances. The post-war corporatist system had confirmed the parliamentary, constitutional route to change as the major strategic orientation of the Left. In this system, governments would use the state to hammer out a compromise between, to borrow a turn of phrase, 'the top floor of the Shell building … the top floor of the Treasury … the top floor of the BBC … [and] the top floor of the TUC'.[43] For mainstream social democracy, the state was the critical actor, holding the ring between rival 'interests'. The task, then, was to elect a Labour government to administer this compromise in a fair way and defend the poorest. But even those in Labour whose objectives were far more radical than the mainstream, tended, for much of the post-war period, to sign up to the essential predicates of this view. The purview of most actually existing socialists involved looking for different ways of using the state to curtail 'the logic of the market'.[44]

This privileging of parliament as the key locus from which change was to be achieved compounded the demoralisation and confusion felt when the corporatist pact began to fall apart, and a New Right espousing a borrowed 'anti-statism' surged. As Britain's underlying economic weaknesses – expressed in declining productivity and profitability – ran confluently into the seventies, leading to rising inflation and unemployment, and as the 1973 OPEC crisis sent the world economy hurtling into the red, the social democratic mainstream, along with a revived Liberal Party, sought to consolidate the role of the interventionist state in securing class compromise. The Labour Left, for its part, did not so much seek to abolish this consensus as effect a sharp shift in the balance of the compromise in favour of workers. Where the corporatist instruments of price and income controls, and the rhetoric of shared sacrifices still prevailed on the Right and centre, Labour's left-wing sought extensive redistribution and nationalisation.

Yet many on the Labour Left and on its periphery also engaged in a thoroughgoing critique of the record of post-war social democracy. As constituency branches and unions moved leftward, members began to critique Harold Wilson's failure to deliver on his manifesto commitments, a fiasco which they blamed for the Conservative's 1970 election victory under Heath.[45] The problem, it was argued, was that Labour had been too timid in confronting concentrated economic and political power. Even where it had nationalised industries, it had left the old guard in charge. In place of deference to parliament and the constitutional settlement, the Left began to advance a critique of the British state and demand democratisation. In addition to extensive nationalisation, and in place of its model of top-down management, they advocated forms of industrial democracy. Tony Benn, a former Gaitskellite who had moved sharply to the left in response to Labour's defeat, played a key role in getting elements of this into Labour's 1974 manifesto. As he argued, his experience as Minister for Technology had shown him the necessity of this as the best means of addressing rising union discontent:

> The old idea of management from the top has got to be looked at again ... the man who actually has to do a job of work on the factory

floor, or in a foundry, or in a shop or office, is the best person to
know how his or her work should be organised … One of the most
horrifying experiences of my ministerial life was to walk round
factories with management that obviously didn't know what was
going on, or who was doing what, and yet quite happily assumed
that the right to manage on behalf of the shareholders included the
right to tell everybody what to do … If we can trust the country
to democracy, why on earth can't we trust individual firms to the
people who work in them? … And if nationalised industries were
seen to be democratically run, and to be distributing incomes more
fairly as well as being accountable to the public for the major decisions they make, we could take a massive step toward democratic
socialism.[46]

Yet the crisis of social democracy would not yield to parliamentary socialism. Instead, as inflation soared, Labour
fell back on traditional corporatist methods to control it.
Working on the theory that excessive wages were driving
up manufacturing costs, which were being passed on
to customers, the Wilson Government elected in 1974
began negotiating a Social Contract with union leaders
that would restrain wage growth to no more than 5 per
cent a year, while inflation greatly exceeded that increase.
While wage growth played a part, not least as organised
labour tried to recoup real-term losses incurred during
the Wilson-era 'balance of payments' crisis, the actual
causes of inflation were considerably more complicated
than the solution of wage-restraint implied. Among the
major causes were soaring global food and energy prices,
coupled with the liberalisation of banking rules under

the Heath administration, which had resulted in a glut of cheap credit.

Nonetheless, there were more fundamental problems, above all a secular decline in profitability and productivity in the manufacturing sector. It was logical that business and their allies in the Bank of England and the Treasury would seek a reduction in wage costs by one means or another, as the first condition for freeing up funds for new investment. Heath had attempted to deal with these structural problems at first by chastening the unions, using the whip of market discipline to enforce competition, and steering Britain into Europe. When Heath's solutions didn't avail, only provoking crippling conflict with the unions, it fell to a Labour government to find a way of reducing the cost of labour with the consent of the labour movement. The problem for social-democratic governments therefore became one of how to achieve wage reductions while finding sufficient *quid pro quo* to secure union acquiescence – a problem that became intractable by 1978, as wildcat strikes signalled the withdrawal of labour's consent to the bargain. Aside from wage restraint, the government also severely reduced public spending under an agreement with the IMF. Unemployment remained at approximately 1 million, a situation for which capital was grateful and – initially – inclined to reward with political support.[47] Amid a frenetic anti-communist clamour in parts of the establishment, and with the Labour Right joining in right-wing press attacks on hate figures on the left such as Tony Benn, civil servants also lobbied Labour leaders to kill off other radical proposals such as Benn's policies for industrial democracy and nationalisation.[48] The centre was falling apart, but the Left singularly lacked the means to take advantage in this hostile terrain.

The Wilderness Years

This is where the New Right found its entrée. As Stuart Hall anticipated in a much-celebrated essay, 'The Great Moving Right Show',[49] the failed attempt to resuscitate the dying body of post-war social democracy merely compounded those aspects of popular discontent with the system that were already destabilising the consensus. The resentments generated by top-down, mandarin control of public industries, by incomes policies, by intrusive welfare bureaucracies and the increasingly authoritarian bent of state interventions may not have been enough by themselves to create a sufficient backlash. But the fact that they manifestly *did not work*, that public enterprises were 'lame ducks', that unemployment still soared, that the consensus had yielded to 'stagflation', and that the social contract broke down with the 'winter of discontent', showed the state to be not merely 'nannying', but also ineffectual. What is more, the leadership of social democracy was increasingly in agreement with the Rightist critique: it was Labour's Denis Healey who effectively introduced the doctrine of 'sado-monetarism' before Thatcher was elected.

In the spaces where social democracy had decomposed, the ideology of Thatcherism began to lay roots. Discovering new energies first unleashed by Enoch Powell, the Conservatives found that a certain 'free market' idiom could gain elements of popular support provided they were linked to the politics of racial backlash.[50] The parlous state of British capitalism could be blamed on an assortment of troublemakers and enemies of order, the migrants, 'muggers' and militants cosseted by a 'creeping socialism': the solution being a dose of old-fashioned British authority, market discipline and, later, firepower. In place of incomes policies and subsidies for lame duck enterprises, Thatcher promised to let crack the whip of the markets. In the car industry, the Tories said, the uncompetitive practices of public ownership and union militancy had led to overmanning and over-priced labour, resulting in cars that could not be sold and rising unemployment. Unions were letting workers down, rather than advancing their interests, while the state supported inefficient industries. Instead, the state should get out of the way, let bad enterprises fail, and let the innovative and industrious succeed. What is more, since the strikes of the era were blamed for inflationary wage claims and had no connection to a wider, popular radical project, their repression could be justified on the grounds that they were narrow, 'selfish' acts harming industrious workers.

Thatcherite discourse struck at a key fault line in social democratic ideology. Social democracy, though emerging from organised labour, cleaved to the possibility of a transcendent national interest, achieved through class compromise and cooperation. This was always going to be difficult to square with the aspirations of its more radical constituents, above all for extensive public ownership of the commanding heights of the economy, in the interests of economic planning. The war state had made a degree of intervention possible, with business happy to cooperate for most of the immediate post-war era, but it was hardly going to persuade the owners of capital to surrender their major sources of profit without a battle. In practice, such aspirations were never on the brink of being realised, but there was at least the prospect that the practice of social democracy would ignite a battle from the other side of the bargain – that of organised labour. This is exactly what had happened in the late seventies, and the New Right seized on this in order to articulate the division in a distinctive way. It was not, they said, a war between classes. The struggle was between the productive and the non-productive. For a 'nation' to be able to afford a welfare system, its productive members had to be taxed, and they would be less inclined to accept this unless the unproductive state and its clients were weaned off the teat.[51]

Thus, the complacent consensus gave way to a belliger-ent offensive led by politicians, intellectuals and institutions largely loyal to the middle-class Right. The flavour of this attack was not to the tastes of the Tory establishment, which largely reacted with horror to Thatcher's vulgar 'retreat behind the privet hedge into the narrow world of class interests and selfish concerns'.[52] Business was also divided over the usefulness of neoliberal nostrums, though a large and dynamic layer of capitalists, led by finance, organised in support of Thatcher's remedies.[53] There was also concern that the ambitious brutality of the government was contributing to an ideological revival of the Labour Left, exemplified by the fact that Tony Benn came within a whisker of defeating Denis Healey in the 1981 election for the deputy leadership. However, whatever excitement Benn was able to generate among constituency activists and a minority of union members, his real support was exaggerated in the election by a system of block voting. A raft of left-wing union leaders had emerged from the previous era of class confrontations, many of whom were inclined to support Benn. But the majority of union members – just like the majority of people – were moving to the right under the pull of Thatcherism. They didn't become Thatcherites, but the gravitational pull was away from the Left. And in the unions that actually balloted all members, Benn was roundly defeated.[54]

The weakness of this Left revival was registered almost immediately when, in March 1981, a faction of the Labour Right organised a split. They had been considering their move for some time. Leading figures in this split, such as Roy Jenkins and David Owen, had been among the pro-government rebels when Heath sought to lead the UK into the European Community. They were infuriated by Wilson's strategy of mediating between the left- and right-wings of Labour, which necessitated that he couldn't campaign for entry on the government's terms. The later calamities of the Wilson/Callaghan government had convinced them that the central problem for social-democratic governance was the power of the trade unions. They argued, just as the Liberals had in the same period, that no party could genuinely govern in the national interest if it was beholden to one class interest. As if this was the only real obstacle faced by the old social-democratic centre. They sought, by ending the Labourist coalition and launching a new party, the Social Democratic Party (SDP), to force an electoral realignment that would draw all the dominant political forces to the centre, and lock the militants and left-wing constituency activists out of power for good.[55]

While the SDP and its Liberal allies were hardly successful in the endeavour to anchor British politics in the centre, the project did build on certain long-term tendencies. The electoral degeneration of the two main post-war parties, the rise of the Liberals and the nationalist parties, and a certain amount of class dealignment in voting,[56] meant that circumstances were ripe for a new electoral calculus. Unfortunately, the immediate beneficiaries were the Conservatives. The popular support for Thatcherism was real enough, however exaggerated by the electoral system.[57] Thatcher had rebounded from the doldrums of 1981 on the basis of a global economic revival beginning in 1982, and in her case linked to martial triumph in the Falklands. But it was the Liberal/SDP alliance which decisively fractured Labour's base, put it on the defensive, ensured that Labour's 1983 vote was the lowest it had gained since 1918, and prevented any recovery until Blair had finally effected the coup de grâce. The 'modernisation' project initiated under Neil Kinnock almost as soon as he was elected leader in 1983, continued by John Smith and consummated by Tony Blair, may have been forced on Labour by other means and in other circumstances. The transformation of social democracy into what has been called 'social liberalism' – a hybrid of traditional social democratic organisation with neoliberal politics – is not peculiar to Britain. It is conceivable that a Left government could have been elected only to see its programme flounder in the face of economic turmoil and resistance from business, thus empowering business-minded 'moderates' to force through a more cautious 'modernisation' agenda. However, without the SDP split, it is difficult to imagine the sweeping scale of the Left's rout in most of its extant quarters of strength, from the miners to municipal socialism. And without the SDP and the victorious Thatcher regime which it enabled, the orchestration of a national witch-hunt and purge of Labour Leftists (above all those said to be tainted by Trotskyism) was not possible.

In the afterglow of the epochal defeats inflicted by Thatcher, it fell to Labour's leadership to detoxify the Labour brand for the liberal middle classes who had deserted it. This project was supported by a union leadership which had swerved sharply to the right, enjoining a 'new realism' according to which unions should seek harmonious relations with all governments, and take a more conciliatory line with employers. This doctrine, unavailing when it was initially unveiled in 1983, proved ideal for a union leadership desperate to avoid conflict after the mauling visited on the miners. And it sufficed for Neil Kinnock, as he and his allies executed an often shambolic, unconvincing retreat from anything which could be considered a left-wing policy, from full employment to unilateral nuclear disarmament.

In a sense, it is difficult to see what else Kinnock could have done. 'Everyone agreed' that these were the steps necessary to make Labour electable, the only worthwhile objective from his point of view. Of course, nothing is ever so simple or so innocent. There were many conceivable ways of being electable, and there was little evidence that the major problem was Labour's core ideological commitments on redistribution, public ownership and welfare. The evidence is that the social attitudes of the majority of people moved significantly *to the left* under Thatcher.[58] Further, the route to electability chosen by the Labour leadership was one congruent with a long-standing strategic perspective on the party's Right, extending back to Gaitskell and company. The problem was that it ultimately meant that Labour dedicated itself to preserving a settlement in which several of the bases of its potential power had been eviscerated. Whatever the 'little caesars of social democracy'[59] may have imagined, Labour's entire basis was the organised working class whom Thatcher had weakened through her fanatical assaults on the industrial base and anti-union laws. Labour and the TUC, however, agreed to accept the majority of the changes wrought by the Tories in the realm of industrial relations. Further, as Labour continued to flounder, it looked for innovative new ways in which it could surrender the instruments of statecraft, ceding one policy area after another to the Thatcherites, such that – accepting the market and competition as the *grundnorms* of any governing politics – it was eventually clear that Labour was left to do little more than humanise what was left to them. Finally, Labour conceded the ideological terrain. In order to explain their electoral difficulties, they began to argue that workers were too comfortably off to support a left-wing programme, too affluent to buy into the language of class solidarity. Left-wing intellectuals who supported the Kinnock leadership fancied that workers had been undergoing a process of 'embourgeoisement'. As Thatcher sought to exclude the very idea of class as a political reference, deriding it as a 'communist concept', Kinnock's team offered a helping hand by replacing such concepts with the market-friendly language of consumers and communities.

By the time Thatcher's reign was finally surrendering to its inner termites, the 'Poll Tax' debacle merely underlining the extent to which her insurgent rightism had become counterproductive for both the business class and her party, Labour's timidity was preventing it from pressing home any advantage handed to it. Thatcher had sought to relieve middle-class taxpayers of as much of the burden of paying for services as possible with the policy of rate-capping. When that initiative reached its limits, the government introduced a Community Charge, a regressive tax that took no account of ability to pay. Here was an issue which suddenly handed Labour majorities, rather than just pluralities, in opinion polls. The voters who had deserted the party to support the SDP–Liberal alliance now appeared ready to return in droves, alongside a swathe of disaffected Conservatives. Labour seemingly had only to remain firm in opposition to the tax in order to preserve the advantage. The problem they faced, however, was that the areas where opposition to the tax was most concentrated were working-class boroughs run by Labour councils. There, the leadership demanded that councils take an unyielding line against non-payment. Just as Neil Kinnock had advocated a 'dented shield' strategy for Labour councils struggling to fund local services in the face of rate-capping, urging that local authorities set strictly legal budgets within the parameters set by the government, so Labour now sought to burnish its constitutionalist credentials by prosecuting non-payers. *The Tribune*, a magazine of the party's soft Left, argued that those Labour members who supported the non-payment campaign represented the 'biggest threat' to Labour's electoral advantage.

Indeed, Labour's commanding poll lead was gradually frittered away, but not because of non-payment. Rather, two developments served to consolidate the Tories' position and allowed alarmed Liberals to return to their party fold. First, John Major replaced Margaret Thatcher as leader, and began to orchestrate a cautious row back from the worst aspects of the Community Charge, while also charting a less confrontational course for the government. While Kinnock attempted to represent Thatcherism-with-a-human-face, he was easily outbid in that necrophilic auction by Major. Second, as in 1982, Britain went to war in Iraq and the response in parliament, the media and much of public opinion was one of jingoistic pride. The majority of Labour MPs, the parliamentary party having rarely passed up on the chance to display its patriotism, were adamantly in favour of the UK's participation in Desert Storm. Only a few opposed with any vim, and the net result was that Major accumulated the political capital of victory in Baghdad without being even slightly inconvenienced by his opposite number.

Labour went into the 1992 election having purged themselves of left-wing policies, centralised power in the hands of the leadership in order to marginalise constituency activists, and embraced modern methods of communication.

With Peter Mandelson and Philip Gould's Shadow Communications Agency setting the tone, they sought to spell out a moderate Labour message, highlighting the need for investment in public services, above all health. As recession ate away at the Tories' economic advantage, and the Community Charge continued to provoke resistance, polls tended to put Labour ahead. Everything was surely in place: Kinnock and his allies had cleaned up the party image, expelled the militants, put manners on the Left, dismantled the last trace of 'municipal socialism', displayed loyalty in war and constitutional integrity in peace, and now stood ready to welcome back prodigal voters. The Conservatives once again returned to government, with their vote barely changed at 42 per cent. Nothing Kinnock had done was adequate to make Labour palatable to southern middle classes, nor to win back the chunks of their old electoral coalition who had defected to the Liberal/SDP alliance after 1981. The party saw only a miserly, 3.6 per cent increase in their vote share. This, for a party which had done everything, gone to all lengths, to expunge any trace of radicalism and accept the terms of its opponents, was a defining trauma. The country, most members seem to have concluded, was just too right-wing for even the most timid reform agenda. It was not clear whether Labour would ever govern again. Wallowing in a sump of defeat, the party was easy prey for the coming Blairite takeover.

The Unavoidable Dilemmas of Social Democracy

For most of the twentieth century, Labour was the unrivalled, mass party of the British working class. Although it never achieved more than two thirds of the working-class vote, no other party of the Left came close to challenging its dominance. Further, barring the Communist Party, which organised a small minority of militants, Labour was the party where most socialists were organised. As such, if the labour movement and their socialist allies largely failed to achieve their far-reaching objectives, the question must be asked as to how Labour has organised and moulded them, and what opportunities it has given members to challenge the status quo.

Without exception, Labour has cleaved to its constitutionalist, electoral roots. It has disowned the radicalism of its members and union affiliates more often than it has allowed them expression. While it has depended on militant members to build and maintain its social movement base, it has excluded them from effective decision-making as far as possible, and in office it has usually taken the lead from civil servants and business. Insofar as it was a coalition between organised labour, socialists and liberals, it has been the union moderates, Fabians and professional liberals who have usually been dominant. It is too simple to characterise Labour as 'the working-class wing of Liberalism', but the liberal legacy has usually been dominant.

Labour's climax, the high point of post-war reform, was achieved in a quite exceptional set of circumstances that were already breaking down by the time the Wilson era was afoot. The availability of business for a class consensus depended both on its need for extensive government intervention to keep capitalism alive and its ability, in the era of national capitalisms, to accept the state as an interlocutor with organised labour. The ability of social democratic governments to deliver reforms in the interests of workers, moreover, depended on an exceptional period of capitalist growth that will probably not be seen again, short of an economic disaster or war that destroys enough capital to create a space for rapid expansion. As soon as that growth no longer obtained, and once the scale of production was sufficiently institutionalised to expose large corporations to competitive pressures that previously had been experienced only by small business, the post-war compromise was doomed.

If it was to survive as a reforming party, Labour needed to find a way to channel popular discontent with the old order – of which it had become the caretaker – into a project to assail the concentrated and increasingly organised power of business. It needed to outflank a popular media that was increasingly dominated by Thatcherism. And it needed to demonstrate that it could offer a new way of doing politics that shrugged off the domesticating constraints of statecraft. Moreover, with the loss of the colonial empire, the rise of Scottish and Welsh nationalisms and the evident shortcomings in parliamentary democracy, the British state was in need of an overhaul which Labour – being wedded to 'Britishness', and the artificial monopoly on left-of-centre political expression that first-past-the-post gave it – was rarely inclined to consider. The Left, for very brief moments, sometimes had the initiative, but never the adequate power, to impose its own solutions. It could never demonstrate sufficient support within the party, let alone in national electoral terms, to transform Labour into a more radical vehicle. And given that the peak of its strategic perspective was the election of Labour governments, it was necessarily trapped by its own logic – a radical left programme rarely has enough support, given normal British psephological realities, to win office. Of course, conditions in Britain today are far from normal. However, even if the radical Left was admitted to government, the evidence is that its real problems would begin at that point. For most of the time, the pressure on Labour has been to move in the opposite direction, not just away from socialism, but increasingly away from the sorts of politics that would once have been mainstream – and that pressure has come from within as much as from without.

The problems that Jeremy Corbyn's team inherits are not just the problems of New Labour's party managers and whips, not just the problems of an enervated 'modernising' project, and not just the problems of a party leadership damaged by the credit crunch. Labour embodies in its make-up and in its traditions, a way of doing politics that for the Left has largely been an experience of failure. For Corbyn to take this institution and transform it into a means to radical inroads on Britain's power systems would require resources, organisation and opportunities that currently don't present themselves. This is not to claim that Corbyn can achieve nothing with this experience, or that his supporters will gain nothing from it. But they are best placed to do so if they are sober about the tremendous obstacles facing them.

4

New Labour and Corbyn's Route to Power

Division among radicals almost 100 years ago resulted in a twentieth century dominated by Conservatives. I want the twenty-first century to be the century of the radicals.

— Tony Blair, almost a century after
the foundation of the Labour Party[1]

He's sold out before he's even got there ... Tax, health, education, unions, full employment, race, immigration ... It won't matter if we win, the bankers and stockbrokers have got us already, by the fucking balls, laughing their heads off.

— Neil Kinnock on Tony Blair[2]

It is, of course, too easy to pin all the blame on the Blairites for the enfeebled Labour Party that Jeremy Corbyn inherited in 2015. But it's nonetheless striking how reluctant they are to take *any* responsibility, or reflect on the fact that they more than anyone else prepared the ground for Corbyn's victory. Asked why she had lost to Corbyn, the Blairite candidate Liz Kendall admitted that her campaign lacked inspiration, suggesting that she had been the 'eat your greens candidate'.[3]

The self-serving nature of such a view is obvious: it says nothing about the record of her political tendency, both in and out of office, and represents the leadership election as a vague battle between sensible moderation and vivid exhortation. But if a relatively unknown candidate from the hard-Left can be so rapidly propelled from nowhere to the top, at a minimum this demands scrutiny of the formerly dominant faction and what they left behind.

What sort of beast was New Labour? Led by Tony Blair, effectively an SDP viper in the Labour breast, it seemed neither entirely new, nor entirely Labour. Yet, the speed and facility with which Blair and his allies took over the party machinery during a few months in 1994, gutted its constitution, banished even a nominal commitment to socialism (the 'marketisation' of Clause Four), at least suggests that this tendency had been incubated within the party for some time. The communitarian moralism abetted by the staccato stock of Blairite conjugations ('rights and responsibilities', 'firm but fair', 'fairness not favours' etc.), was not entirely novel. Nor were the 'ethical' pieties, the liberal cynosures or the elevation of 'nation' above 'class'. The Labour Left was outmanoeuvred on every front, resigning itself to the miserable hope that government would at least allow a mitigation of the worst of Toryism, yet it seemed at all points to inhabit roughly the same party as before.

Few left-wingers expected what was to come; that even those policy nostrums with which New Labour defined itself in opposition – for example, opposition to Private Finance Initiatives, resistance to Michael Howard's anti-immigrant legislation, or reversing the sell-off of Air Traffic Control – would be ditched once government was secured. Far less could they anticipate the vindictive attacks on welfare, targeting single mothers and the disabled, or the revival of that old familiar tincture of moral imperialism in alliance with a right-wing US administration. But there was little sign of organised rebellion against these policies within the party. Did that signify that Labour as it had once existed no longer did, or that the party had just returned to some very old, recognisable Labour roots?

There was at least one thing that could be said for the claim of novelty on Blair's part. If Labour's relationship to the working class had always been complicated, New Labour – like the Oedipal child – sought to deny its own vulgar parentage, and disown as far as possible the movement which gave birth to it. Blair often gave the impression that he thought the very formation of Labour as a party separate from Liberalism had been a mistake. He seemed to want to break Labour's founding relationship with organised labour, and to create a party much like the Democratic Party in the United States to whom the unions could plead for favours like any other client. In that sense, New Labour could be seen simply as the triumph of an old, predominantly middle-class liberal current, previously led by Roy Jenkins. Yet, Blair did not succeed in breaking the union link, and the unions did not act against him. Whatever was new about New Labour, it remained in some vital respects a very traditional social democratic party.

And what should not be missed is that, however much New Labour now stands condemned in the eyes of most Labour members and voters, it once conveyed power and purpose, and intellectual conviction, something that was extremely seductive for the traumatised survivors of four successive Tory election victories. Tens of thousands of members, and many more voters, appear to have been genuinely enthused by New Labour – easy to forget, in an era when Blairite MPs look and sound like dull building society managers.

New Labour in Theory and Practice

New Labour strategists and intellectuals are sometimes given to borrowing the language and concepts of the Sardinian Marxist Antonio Gramsci. Among the key ideas they took from Gramsci was the concept of 'hegemony', which is a form of power that goes beyond force and violence. A hegemonic group doesn't just dominate, it sets a moral agenda, it is ideologically persuasive, and it draws others toward it by taking their interests into account. In Gramsci's terms, this was intended to be an explanation for how industrial workers could win leadership in a broad class alliance with peasants and others. But for New Labour intellectuals, it came to refer to a narrow party-political objective, of shaping an electoral agenda and winning a parliamentary majority. The justifications for New Labour as a successful 'hegemonic' project[4] coming from the likes of former health secretary John Reid and former Blair speech-writer Peter Hyman are not, in this sense, a one-off. The intellectual origins of New Labour can be traced, in part, to an assortment of soft-left intellectuals, many of them either residing in the Communist Party or in its orbit, and usually writing for the journal *Marxism Today*.[5]

These ranged from heavyweights such as cultural theorist Stuart Hall and historian Eric Hobsbawm, to figures such as management guru Charles Leadbeater and policy adviser Geoff Mulgan. Espousing a version of Gramscian Marxism, they tended to argue that the foundations of the old Left – which they derided as economistic, class-reductionist, expecting militant revival at every turn – had been eroded in the post-war world and were now being blown away by global capitalism. Even at the peak of socialist consciousness, they argued, the British working class had never been as unanimously left-wing as its continental equivalents. And now with the rise of consumerist individualism, the decline of trade union organisation and the decay of the old social democratic order, the radical right was expanding the fill the spaces that neither socialism nor social democracy seemed able to. Thatcherism could tap into certain popular pleasures in the market, while mobilising popular discontent with the social democratic state.

In all, they noted, a great shift in capitalist civilisation had taken place. Economies were now global rather than national, the mass media was increasingly tending toward twenty-four-hour coverage, the working class was fragmenting and identities were increasingly plural. These changes, they collectively labelled 'New Times'.[6] And in these 'New Times', a Left that stuck to the old remedies could not win 'hegemony' in the working class, let alone command across a broad class alliance for socialism. It was on this basis that they led a vitriolic charge against the hard-Left, seeking their exclusion in a realignment of forces for a modernised Left.[7]

Though much of what the *Marxism Today* intellectuals said was luminous and prescient, above all when it came with Hall's suave, seductive and assured voice, at least a similar quotient was charlatanry, bullshit and self-fulfilling prophesy. The critique of the Left's cultural oblivious-ness, the theorisation of a new capitalism and the role of consumption and new forms of individualism in it, segued often into a kind of cheerleading for this new state of affairs and the bold energies it seemed to unleash. If Stuart Hall and Martin Jacques could recognise the danger of a Labour Government embracing a 'brand of New Times' that was just a 'slightly cleaned up' version of the radical Right, this was in part because their own intellectual project was a little too entranced by Thatcherite dynamism, and a great deal too scornful of Thatcher's most belligerent opponents. And although these same intellectuals would later reject New Labour as a form of warmed-over Thatcherism, it is well to remember that they had initially welcomed Blair and his reforming zeal.[8]

What became the intellectual foundation of New Labour, then, was in some respects a dilute rip-off of the most vacuous elements of 'New Times' thinking – above all the celebration of designer global capitalism. And indeed, some of the leading figures from that intellectual milieu, such as Mulgan and Leadbeater, were integrated into the New Labour policymaking elite. Another crucial phase of New Labour thinking was pivoted on the ideas associated with the sociologist Anthony Giddens and his prospectus for a 'Third Way', 'beyond left and right'. For Giddens, the centre-Left had to abandon ideas of redistribution, and the traditional uses of welfare. It had to abandon equality for meritocracy, wherein the role of the state would be to attack the forms of exclusion that prevented people from participating fully in meritocratic competition. It had to embrace consumption as a key means by which people organised their identities. It had to accept globalisation as a necessary process, while seeking to manage the risks. Perhaps Giddens's most distinctive contribution was to argue that the relationship between the welfare state and the class structure had fundamentally changed. 'Welfare dependency', that reactionary old cliché, was dusted down in Giddens's account and given a centre-left gloss. Instead of welfare being a safety net to prevent poverty in the event of market failure, it had increasingly become an impediment to people getting out of poverty, and a means of social exclusion. Welfare thus had to be reformed in order to lever people out of this dependency and into paid work. One of the key ideas embraced by Tony Blair in an effort to stress the novelty of New Labour, therefore, was that of 'workfare' – an idea that came with a distinctive note of moralism, as the emphasis shifted from welfare as a citizenship right, to welfare as a privilege gained in exchange for proving certain moral bona fides such as a willingness to work.

There is also the distinctive formation of Blair himself to take into account. Although he had claimed in correspondence to Michael Foot that he 'came to Socialism through Marxism',[9] it seems rather unlikely that he had ever come within a country mile of either. Nothing he has ever said or done indicates the presence of such formative influences, and the most realistic explanation seems to be Labour historian Martin Pugh's, that Blair entered politics 'as an impressionable and largely non-political young man', that he gravitated to those with power and success, and that his attraction to 'fairly extreme right-wingers' such as Bush, Berlusconi, Aznar and Sarkozy was in part a reflection of his formation in a Conservative family and in part a reflection of his susceptibility to power.[10]

One of the things that was meant by New Labour, moreover, was that it was a fundamentally different kind of party to that which had been known. As the former *Marxism Today* intellectuals astutely argued, Labour had been 'running, ever since Neil Kinnock's election to the leadership, mainly against itself. Key speeches to party and trade union audiences have nearly always emphasised departures from traditional party thinking, and taken the form of public demonstrations ... of how different New Labour was from what had gone before'.[11] The dramatic dropping of one social-democratic nostrum after another was the main policy mood music, culminating in the symbolic change to Clause IV of the constitution, wherein the rigours of the market were to be the main instrument of delivering fairness. But the party itself also had to change.

The centre of power in the Labour Party had never been the constituency membership. In the party's classically federal structure, in which individual members were one component alongside trade unions and various socialist societies, the main power had traditionally been invested in the union leaders. At national conference, after 1918, unions had cast 2,471,000 votes, as compared to 115,000 cast by constituency branches, and 48,000 cast by socialist societies. Through the first experiences of office, the weight of power began to shift to the parliamentary leadership, but this didn't necessarily trouble the union leadership, which understood the need for firm party management, and whose interests were usually congruent with those of the party elite. What is more, managers of both unions and the party tended to converge on their view of the constituency membership as a control problem, being filled with middle-class idealists and unreliable socialists. They were useful to connect to the electorate, but otherwise to be kept away from decision-making.[12] Hence, unions for most of the twentieth century provided the party leadership with a reliable ally, and ensured the unshakeable dominance of the Right and centre over the party machinery.

This was the core of the old Labour Right's power in the organisation. But it had begun to slowly enter into a crisis in the 1960s, in part because the union leaderships began to move to the left, and in part because the social-democratic compact was breaking down. By the 1970s, a section of the party's right-wing was convinced that unions themselves were the problem, rather than their best ally. And by the early 1980s, the party had seen several union leaders line up behind Tony Benn's radical socialist candidacy for deputy leader. Not only that, but thanks to the trade union influence, the National Executive Committee, traditionally controlled by the party's right-wing, had been increasingly populated by the Left – something that the right-wing backlash of the 1980s had only partially succeeded in fixing.[13] The new Labour Right wanted a different kind of power base and, to that purpose, had been enjoying a longing look abroad, at the Democratic Party of the United States. The 'American Tendency' in the Labour Party, as it was dubbed by Robin Ramsay, had always been strong, but it was in the course of early 1990s junkets funded by US businesses that Blair and Brown had begun to forge their alliances with the 'New Democrats'.[14] There was a party in which a dynamic layer of 'New Democrats' was coming to the fore, ready to swing their party hard to the right and bring the grass-roots activists to heel, in order to win. There, the unions had their proper place: as subordinate clients, donors who might be able to buy a few concessions but who had little say in policymaking or internal power struggles. The founders of New Labour convinced themselves and those around them that the union influence in the Labour Party had been a major cause of the party's ongoing electoral difficulties, despite psephological studies providing little evidence for this.[15]

Blair and his allies – Mandelson, Brown, Campbell, and Gould – set about radically reorganising the Labour Party and transferring power to the top and centre of the organisation. The first change was to consolidate the powers of the leadership, which was seen as both an electoral asset insofar as it helped project Blair's telegenic image. It was also construed as being more democratic, insofar as the leadership would be more responsive to popular opinion, as gauged in polls and focus groups, than the unrepresentative party membership. Finally, it would help the leadership secure the support of business and the City, if the membership were seen to be under firm control. The second major change was to the annual conference. Increasingly stage-managed debates took the place of actual policymaking, which was shifted to the National Policy Forum. This was linked to the third change, in which the union block vote was replaced with a voting procedure inaccurately dubbed 'One Member One Vote' (OMOV). In fact, the new system was based on an electoral college in which each MP's vote had the same weight as thousands of members votes. A genuine OMOV system was not used until the 2015 leadership election. Alongside these constitutional changes, the Blairites proved extremely adept at managing and neutralising NEC discussions, and intervening in selection procedures for parliamentary candidates. With the internal lobby group Progress backing them up and with funding from Lord Sainsbury, they successfully parachuted candidates in to safe seats, to ensure that the parliamentary party more closely aligned with the leadership.[16]

The scale of the changes wrought in Labour were all the more remarkable because the actual number of Blairites in the party, even in the parliamentary party, was quite small. The pro-Blair columnist Martin Kettle estimated the number in parliament at perhaps a dozen MPs.[17] They were always operating as a minority vanguard, and would not have been

remotely as effective had it not been for the demoralisation
of the entire party. Yet, in their way, they merely continued
the lines of political and organisational change already signalled under Neil Kinnock, whose hoarding of leadership
power and attempt to isolate and disempower the constituency and union base in the interests of 'electability' was the
prototype upon which Blair's reign was fashioned.[18]

New Labour in Power

While the Blairites adapted Labour culturally, politically and organisationally to the success of Thatcherism,
there had been a growing revolt against it among some
of its former supporters, particularly after a major economic debacle in 1992, in which the Major administration
attempted to pilot Britain into the European Exchange
Rate Mechanism (ERM), only to find it had to support the
currency's value with soaring interest rates. This underlined the economic insecurity that the Conservatives had
brought even to some traditionally comfortable middle-
class layers. Almost nothing in the interim between 'Black
Wednesday' in 1992, when the UK crashed out of the
ERM, and the general election in May 1997, altered or
reversed the huge shift in a critical section of the electorate. The Conservatives languished at around 30 per cent
in the polls, while Labour tended to poll in the low forties.
Labour's biggest gains in 1997 were among (white-collar
and middle-class) AB voters, while it actually saw a small
decline in its support from ('unskilled' and unemployed)
DE voters.

What New Labour would do with power was not entirely clear at this point. In an era in which the very power of national governments to deliver reforms was under question, the Blairites gainsaid the question. The traditional range of reforms was barely aimed for, while the word 'reform' itself was captured for purposes entirely contrary to social-democratic traditions: for example, the application of market 'efficiency' to even those treasured and sentimentalised achievements of Labour's past. The legacy inherited by the incoming government was bleak. At the foundation was an economy that lacked competitiveness, whose share of global trade had plummeted, and whose manufacturing base was withering. The UK economy was disproportionately pivoted on finance and commerce, something that the Major administration had struggled to rectify but without the requisite policy instruments. In the interstices of economic decline there had arisen unprecedented levels of poverty and, despite the increasingly broad diffusion of multicultural sensibilities, much of it was concentrated among ethnic minorities who had been forced into urban enclaves by a combination of council policy and white racism. Income inequality had risen faster in the UK than in any comparable industrialised country. In the rush to home ownership and sales of council housing, the housing stock had been left to crumble in large areas of the country. The falling value of pensions meant that a growing number of pensioners were in poverty.[19]

New Labour's instrument for dealing with this legacy was what Gordon Brown called 'post-monetarist economics'. This entailed a rejection of Keynesian demand-management techniques, and an acceptance of the doctrine of the 'non-accelerating inflation rate of unemployment' (NAIRU), according to which spending to create jobs was likely to drive up inflation to unsustainable levels. Mainstream economists argued that the 'natural' rate of unemployment was approximately 5 per cent. Brown's strategy was to reduce that level through supply-side measures intended to make hiring more attractive to employers. This could be done by reducing taxes on profits, cutting taxes on employment and even subsidising employment in certain conditions. It also involved maintaining strong anti-union laws to reduce the bargaining power of labour, investing to increase the skills and productivity of workers. Gordon Brown, recognising this, placed particular emphasis on skilling up labour.

Thus, New Labour reduced corporation taxes and small business taxes, kept most of the anti-union laws in place, and introduced various schemes such as the 'New Deal' which were intended to skill-up workers and pay employers to give them work experience. There is not much evidence of success on this front. Employment rose, in general, despite continued low productivity, and expansion was predicated on low-skilled labour.[20] Aside from this, there was little progressive about such supply-side strategies. Improving workers' skills may be a good strategy for business but, on its own, would simply raise the supply of skilled workers and thus depress the cost of labour. And indeed, the imperative to keep labour cheap and flexible shaped and limited many of the measures Labour implemented to satisfy their base — a minimum wage was introduced in the spring of 1999 but at a pitiably low level of £3.60 for adults, some of the worst anti-union controls were repealed but the majority were kept in place, and Labour continued to seek UK opt-outs from EU labour codes.

Spending was also constrained by the promise that taxes on higher income earners and company profits would be kept low, such that corporation tax was cut from the first budget. Further, borrowing was constrained by Gordon Brown's 'golden rule' identified in his first budget – 'over the economic cycle the Government will borrow only to invest'.[21] Given the attempts by Conservatives to claim that Labour 'overspending' produced the deficit – barely contested by Labour – it is important to outline the facts of how Blair and Brown managed spending. In New Labour's first term, from 1997 to 2001, the top priority was not public investment but establishing credibility with financial markets by reducing government debt. The debt was reduced by a total of £34bn in the last year of New Labour's first term – a larger total reduction than all the cumulative debt reduction of previous governments for fifty years. This meant that investment in most government departments fell precipitously for the first years of the New Labour administration. Overall public spending fell from over 40 per cent of GDP in 1997 to 38.1 per cent in 2001. Even with successive fiscal problems in the ensuing years and a subsequent need to borrow to plug black holes, by 2004 Gordon Brown had reduced the debt from 44 per cent of national income to 34 per cent. By 2005, the combined spending on debt interest and unemployment benefits had fallen by a half. In the latter half of the 2000s, public spending would rise to above 40 per cent again, reaching 41.1 per cent in 2007–08. Only with the credit crunch and ensuing recession did it return to levels last seen in Thatcher's first two terms, rising to 47.5 per cent of GDP for 2009–10. The deficit that arose resulted from the reduction in the tax base as unemployment soared and the economy shrank, along with the massive bailouts for the financial sector.[22]

Nor could such investment as was provided be disaggregated from the wider policy framework guiding its use. It was one thing for the government to boast of monies for new hospitals and schools, but the most immediately obvious and visible way that it chose to invest these was in futile semi-privatisation schemes, in which private contractors were given lucrative thirty-year contracts to build and maintain services at greatly inflated cost, and with significantly reduced services.[23] Finally, and most importantly, the entire model of investment depended upon the economic growth provided by a booming financial sector and soaring consumer spending. As soon as that growth model no longer availed, the basis for New Labour's cautious experiments in social democracy was gone.

Work, Flag and Family

The government's economic policy dovetailed with a social moralism that shaped both its welfare and its penal policies. Since, after all, the government was providing 'opportunity' and removing the sources of 'exclusion', any lingering resistance to inclusion on these terms had to be the result of welfare dependency or other behaviours needing discipline. As Gordon Brown put it in his first budget, anticipating the current government's language on workfare, since Labour was offering young people the chance of paid work or training, 'benefits will be cut' for anyone refusing to 'take up the opportunities'. This was also related to the government's obsession with proving its pro-family bona fides. Like any Conservative, Blair tended to locate the blame for social problems in the decay of the family. In Mandelson and Liddle's account of the formation of New Labour, they quote Blair's explanation of the Jamie Bulger killing that it was undoubtedly a result of the 'breakdown in family life'. Later, the government would also add the string of 'Britishness' to its bow, arguing that to be included was to be integrated into a core of – always vaguely defined – British values. This produced a strange effect. On the face of it, New Labour was cosmopolitan, socially progressive and averse to bigotry. Its abolition of Section 28, opposed by Conservatives who would blush to admit it today, seemed to signal the arrival of, dixit John Major, 'a nation at ease with itself'. Yet in many respects New Labour's model of social inclusion, guided by the virtues of work, flag and family, reflected the social values of a provincial fifties suburb.[24]

Social policy under New Labour put a premium on the promotion of 'paid work' as the critical means of social inclusion. The shift on the spectrum from welfare to workfare, part of a long-developing consensus among governing elites since the 1980s, was necessarily also a shift from safety net to discipline. Surprisingly, despite cleaving to social values more typically liberal than Blair's, the centre-left press was at times an important ally for New Labour on

this front. For example, when Blair, shortly before his resignation, planned policies cutting welfare for jobless single
parents and introducing agencies to 'nudge' benefits claim-
ants back to work, the *Observer* was there to cast this as
another example of Blair's magic rapport with some mythi-
cal, mysterious creature named 'Asda Woman'.[25] Likewise,
when the government first floated workfare – later implemented fully as a Conservative policy – the liberal columnist
Polly Toynbee was among its most vociferous champions:
'The Tories were right,' she announced, 'workfare really
works.'[26] Nor did Labour stop once it had started. Having
immediately cut benefits for single mothers after being
elected with a landslide, in a policy graciously left to Harriet
Harman to steward through parliament, it was soon going
after the disabled and future retirees. Cynically, one might
applaud such measures if they did 'work' on their own
terms. In fact, where New Labour did succeed in reducing forms of poverty it was through surreptitious forms of
spending and targeted benefits increases.[27] Total employment continually climbed until the credit crunch, but there
is no evidence that benefit cuts or the threat thereof had any
significant impact.

In addition to welfare cuts and inducements to take paid
employment, the government looked for ways to discipline and erase forms of bad behaviour that it claimed were
eroding families and communities and contributing to
social exclusion. With curfews and Anti-Social Behaviour
Orders, the government set about criminalising otherwise
perfectly lawful behaviour. Often the law was strange and
nasty in application: a boy with Tourette's syndrome was

given an ASBO for swearing. Another man was threatened with an ASBO for joking about the death of the Pope. A boy was ASBOd for the grievous offence of wearing a hoodie. And as if to underline just how callous and perverse the law was, a woman with noted suicidal tendencies was given an ASBO forbidding her from going near railway lines or multistorey car parks.[28] The definition of 'anti-social behaviour' was so vague that practically any behaviour could be subject to such an order, and any citizen could thus end up threatened with prison for non-compliance. New Labour developed such confidence in its measures that, toward the end of his reign, Blair began to suggest that the government could pre-emptively intervene to prevent the children of problem families from becoming a 'menace to society' – a form of intervention that could even take place 'pre-birth'.[29] Finally, if parents of children acting 'anti-socially' refused government help, there were to be 'parenting orders' mandating forcible state intervention to nudge them along.[30]

This was linked to two developments, one in the scale of repression, and one in the tenor of popular culture. First, to enforce the new disciplinary order, police numbers, as well as the rate of imprisonment in the UK, both soared under New Labour. Thatcher increased police numbers from just shy of 110,000 to approximately 125,000. Under Major, police numbers remained relatively flat. Under New Labour, police numbers increased from 125,051 in March 1997 to 141,631 in March 2010.[31] The prison population almost doubled from 44,386 in June 1993 to 86,048 in June 2012.[32] One notable result of all this was a surge in prison overcrowding and a dramatic increase in prison riots and hostage-taking in jails.[33] Second, under New Labour the consensus on welfare and redistribution shifted sharply to the right.[34] The demonisation of the poor, the rise of stereotypes about council estate dwellers, single mothers, 'feral' teens and 'chavs' was the logical terminus to which New Labour's ideological thrust moved Britain – and on such terrain, neither the Tories nor UKIP have had much difficulty making gains.

Logically enough, Blair's particular emphasis on the institution of the family also segued into a racial authoritarianism, as in his final days in office he decided to leave his mark by identifying 'black culture' as the cause of a series of knife and gun murders in the capital: 'we won't stop this by pretending it isn't young black kids doing it'. In particular, New Labour was concerned that the breakdown of black family life had given rise to a generation of children without appropriate parental discipline. Here, the government once again pushed the boundaries of debate to the right, helped along by some in the race relations industry, such as the New Labour-friendly Commission for Racial Equality, who backed Blair's speech.[35] There had developed, since the 1980s, a consensus on multiculturalism and anti-racism which for all its flaws had constrained previous Conservative administrations. In an effort to render race a politically manageable problem, the discourse of multiculturalism sought to create a well-defined representational space for each 'culture', wherein selected representatives of each supposedly discrete entity would be given access to funding and influence in exchange for their role in securing political quiescence.

Though New Labour had no intention of rowing back from the practice, the cultural consensus it produced posed certain problems for a government seeking to outflank the Tories on the issue of immigration, and subsequently to discipline British Asians following the 2001 northern riots. Jack Straw, as Home Secretary, cheerfully vilified Roma gypsies as troublemakers who 'think that it's perfectly OK for them to cause mayhem in an area, to go burgling, thieving, breaking into vehicles, causing all kinds of other trouble including defecating in the doorways of firms and so on'.[36] Notably, the invocation of misplaced excrement as a symptom of multicultural disorder had previously found its way into Enoch Powell's 'Rivers of Blood' speech.

Later, in setting up a network of detention centres for asylum seekers and replacing cash benefits with stigmatising vouchers, Straw went further than the previous Home Secretary Michael Howard had dared. Those detention centres have notoriously become routine sites of human rights abuses. David Blunkett demanded that British Asians should speak English in their own homes, proposed a 'Britishness test' for immigrants, and signalled that 'multiculturalism' was over. New Labour-friendly intellectuals, such as David Goodhart and Trevor Phillips, gave this ideological shift a neo-Powellite gloss, drawing on the culturalist racism of the New Right. Phillips declared multiculturalism over, demanding of minorities 'integration' to shared values which were always just on the brink of being discovered. Goodhart argued that the existence of wide varieties of people culturally too dissimilar undermined the basis for the welfare state, since few would willingly pay

into the pot to help people who were different: 'most of us
prefer our own kind'.[37] In place of many cultures, there was
to be 'Britishness' and a demand that all 'cultures' assimilate to this core of national being. In place of challenging
racism and the disadvantages it brought to minorities,
there was to be victim-blaming, and unfounded claims
that British Asians were 'self-segregating'.[38] As all of this
took place, unsurprisingly, so did a renewed surge in racist
violence and harassment. Between 1996 and 1997 and 2003
and 2004, racial incidents more than quadrupled in England
and Wales from 13,151 in 1996–97 to 52,694.[39]

Disillusionment and Demoralisation

As Labour approached the 2001 general election, Blair was
in a characteristically strident mood. Everywhere, opinion
polls told him that his major policy of public sector reform,
the Private Finance Initiative (PFI), was deeply unpopular.
Analyses suggested that such policies were costly boondog-
gles giving favoured private enterprises access to grotesque
amounts of public money for new hospitals and schools or
renovations that were far more cheaply done in the public
sector. Worse, they resulted in poorer services, as PFI hospitals tended to have fewer staff and fewer beds. In every
conceivable respect, the policy was a disaster.[40] Labour was
no longer just running against itself and its own social-
democratic instincts. It was also running against the British
public, to the extent that they shared those instincts. Blair
decided that PFIs were not just another policy, but were
the flagship policy for this election, and dared the electorate

to oppose him. Of course, given that PFI was originally a Conservative policy, there was little to choose between the big two parties on this issue. Only in one constituency, the marginal Kidderminster seat of Wyre Forest, was a candidate for the makeshift party Health Concern able to capitalise on opposition to PFI and take the seat from Labour. But elsewhere, much of the electorate simply abstained. Turnout plunged to below 60 per cent for the first time since 1918. The biggest drop was in the Labour vote, which fell by just short of 3 million, while the Tory vote dropped by just over a million.

The disillusionment even spread into the quarters of the old Labour Right. Former deputy-leader Roy Hattersley, who can be credited with laying some of the groundwork for New Labour, declared that under Blair the party had not only moved further and ever faster to the right, but had embraced 'an alien ideology'. By replacing the discourse of equality with that of 'meritocracy', it had in effect signed up to 'shifting patterns of inequality'.[41] Urging party members to 'rise up against the coup d'état' against social democracy, he committed himself to an unavailing fight against the Blairites – apparently oblivious of the fact that the battle against the Left, in which he had energetically participated, had also helped decimate the ranks of almost all currents to the left of New Labour within the party. If he now found that old Rightists like him were marginalised, how much more so were the soft Left who had once formed common cause with him? In initiating the reforms of the party structure which centralised more power in the hands of party managers in order to sideline constituency activists, they empowered the clique whose ascension they had done so much to bring about. And in driving out or demoralising some of the most confident and capable militants in the interests of electability, and by forcing through the party's adaptation to Thatcherism, they had compounded the traumas which made the grass roots so susceptible to the Blairite takeover. Unsurprisingly then, none of the grumblings of discontent amounted to a serious challenge to the leadership.

It is quite possible that developments in the trade unions might have led to a rupture in other circumstances. On 11 September 2001, Blair was due to give a speech to delegates at the TUC conference, at which it was expected that he would be given a rough ride over his unseemly determination to force through private sector involvement in public services. There had been, alongside a growing discontent among trade unionists, the beginnings of an ideological radicalisation among a layer of young people, manifest in the anti-capitalist movements. Public opinion, after a series of disasters in the rail network, was overwhelmingly calling for renationalisation.[42] New Labour had failed to secure victory for its London mayoral candidate against the left-of-centre challenger, Ken Livingstone, who was pledged to oppose the Public Private Partnership (PPP) on the Underground.[43] Small chinks in the armour of neo-liberal rule were beginning to open up. Whatever may have happened, however, the attacks on the World Trade Center suddenly shifted the conversation to other matters, and secured a quiet welcome for Blair.[44] While the government remained determined to press ahead with policies that would leave transport, health and education services paying off huge dividends to corporations for decades into the future, the emphasis shifted to the prime minister's allegiance with President Bush, and the wars that were to come.

Public opposition to the first such war, in Afghanistan, was seemingly muted – but already, unexpectedly large public protests signalled what was to come.[45] By the late summer of 2002, as Blair prepared to lead his party to war in Iraq, up to 400,000 people had demonstrated in London.[46] Significantly for New Labour, the build-up to war divided the traditionally pro-Labour press, as the *Mirror* came out against the prime minister while the *Observer* remained fiercely loyalist[47] – even to the point of suppressing explosive stories developed by its leading journalists, such as the news that the CIA considered Bush's 'weapons of mass destruction' line to be a pack of lies, or that the United States had been spying on the UN Security Council. By early February 2003, Blair was faced with the largest popular opposition he had yet faced, with overwhelming opposition to the looming Iraq War signalled by the presence of approximately a million anti-war demonstrators in London.[48] This anti-war movement was remarkable for the fact that, despite the prominence of seasoned Labour left-wingers such as Tony Benn, George Galloway and, of course, Jeremy Corbyn, its massed ranks drew as much from the affluent and professional suburbanites as from the metropolitan Left. Blair drew upon his immense reserves of contumely for public error to issue a counterblast as imperious as it was self-serving. It was, he remarked, wonderful that people could protest in a democracy, much as they could not in Iraq. But in addition to rooting out weapons of mass destruction which Saddam had allegedly concealed in a series of wily desert escapades, the war would bring liberation to an oppressed people. He did not 'seek unpopularity as a badge of honour. But sometimes it is the price of leadership. And the cost of conviction'.[49] As is often the case when political leaders scorn popular will, he evinced a matchless heroism about his purpose, as if true courage was to defend a cause with no more powerful allies than the Ministry of Defence, the major press and broadcasters, the Pentagon, the CIA and the White House.

The presidentialism of Blair's leadership style was exacerbated by his foreign policy belligerence. The role of the prime minister in prosecuting wars is inevitably far greater than in the execution of domestic policy, and Blair did not hesitate to take advantage of this. He was inordinately fond of being seen on the international stage, with world leaders, or among military men, with white shirt-sleeves rolled up, as if he was about to throttle an enemy combatant himself. This Blair, who had proved even more belligerent than a centrist US president in waging Operation Desert Fox in Iraq, and the Kosovo War, who aligned with a hard right US president in the invasion of Iraq, and whose astonishing zeal in battling Labour's own supporters now took the form of facing down a mass social movement which went from the inner city estates to the heart of cherished 'Middle England', was the Blair whom much of the commentariat fell in love with.

If there had been any expectation that the dominance

of New Labour would suddenly prove depthless, that the grass roots would rebel, or even that there would be a left-wing split on the model of Continental equivalents – where the senior defections led to the formation of new radical left parties – it was disappointed. While Labour Party activists partook fully in the peak of anti-war activity in 2002 and 2003, and Labour banners were even occasionally visible on protests, the party as a whole remained strikingly cohesive. Despite resignations of senior ministers such as Robin Cook, and despite deep unhappiness on the backbenches about the case for war, only one Labour MP would find himself on the outside of the party after the war began. This was George Galloway, who did not choose to leave but was driven out over comments urging Iraqis to fight the invaders and calling on troops to defy orders. Galloway's exit enabled a short-lived alliance of the far Left and Muslim groups to form on an anti-war, left-wing platform, and the political party they formed, Respect, was able to embarrass Labour with a stunning swing in a core East End constituency, while taking sizeable numbers of votes in Birmingham and Leicester. Yet such a ramshackle, federal alliance, overly dominated by certain well-placed egos, was never likely to seriously challenge Labour's heartland dominion on a broader basis, even as its working-class vote eroded.

Meanwhile, the Labour Party conference in 2003 was remarkable for one thing – the absence of Iraq from the discussion, and the torrents of standing ovations for one right-wing speech after another. John Reid was cheered to the rafters for a speech promising to model the NHS on private health provision. David Blunkett roused conference with a speech attacking the Liberal Democrats from the populist Right on crime: 'they know just where they stand. Four square behind the human rights of the perpetrator'.[50] And to cap it all, Tony Blair won seven minutes of applause for a classical strident performance culminating in the line, 'I've not got a reverse gear'. All of this was manna for the constituency activists, who didn't have to be hectored into such extraordinary displays of loyalty. Their fervour was reflected in their votes. As Nick Cohen wrote in the *Observer*: 'Activists from constituency Labour parties usually backed Blair by a majority of three-to-one. The majority never fell below two-to-one, however contentious the issue. From now on when the whips confront a rebellious Labour backbencher, they will be able to tell him he isn't standing up for his local party workers but flying in the face of their express wishes.'[51]

One of the main reasons the war did not enter the formal debate that year was because the unions played their traditional role in protecting the party leadership on its most exposed flank, using their block votes to prevent a motion on the war from being debated. This is not to say that the unions were happy with the government. The union leaderships acted to spare the government's blushes, because they saw it as 'their' government. However, New Labour ministers seemed to take glee in attacking them and inciting their outrage. Health Minister John Reid was particularly combative in his speech supporting 'foundation hospitals', a matter on which he knew the unions would vote against him. It didn't matter, since conference had long since lost any serious policymaking authority, and Reid could declare that even if he lost the vote to the unions, he had 'won the argument'. But, while handing the government empty defeats on public sector reform, any motion on war was kept off the agenda, so that Defence Secretary Geoff Hoon could deliver a pro-war sermon to polite applause.[52]

Discontent with New Labour among union leaders therefore bubbled away, with occasional empty threats to withdraw funding or seek out a new political partner, leading to short-lived confrontations which usually fizzled out before a major breach. One such confrontation came to a head in the year after the Iraq War began, over Blair's determination to persist with Private Finance Initiatives and market-based public sector 'reform'. But any chance of this becoming an organised breach between the union leadership and the party leadership was neutralised by the decision of the National Policy Forum in Warwick to offer the unions a series of incentives to remain in the fold. The offer was modest, comprising some employment rights such as restrictions on firing striking workers, and a promised review on the gender pay gap.[53] But this was the classic *quid pro quo* for the unions – squeezing for reforms in exchange for loyalty within the overarching policy framework.

With this agreement under its belt, the anti-war movement still powerful but receding, and the Tories still stuck with an unpopular Thatcher-era relic as their leader, New Labour could go into the next general election with a war treasury supplied by the unions. Despite the localised threats posed by Respect and various anti-war campaigns, the major beneficiaries of Labour's losses, with almost a further million votes gone, were the Liberal Democrats, whose personable and highly regarded leader had taken a wanly anti-war stance for as long as it was convenient.

Brown Fudge

Notwithstanding Blairite obduracy, greatly inflamed in the aftermath of the attacks on London on 7 July 2005 – upon which, Blair gravely informed us, the rules of the game had changed – the beginning of the end of New Labour was becoming gradually visible. There was, for a start, an increasingly broad constituency of left-wingers, liberals, middle-of-the-road Conservatives, and those of a libertarian persuasion, for whom New Labour's statist authoritarianism seemed to be out of control. The extremely broad uses to which anti-terrorist legislation was put, pre-empting the way in which different groups of protesters under Conservative rule were stigmatised as 'terrorist' and 'extremists',[54] was the softer end of a continuum of authoritarian policies that extended through CCTV on Muslim council estates to extraordinary rendition.[55] Twinned with this was a rising arc of Islamophobic provocation from the government and friendly intellectuals. Jack Straw's gratuitously public refusal to speak to Muslim constituents in Blackburn who wore the full veil merely punctuated an increasingly febrile climate that led *Guardian* columnist Jonathan Freedland to opine: 'If this onslaught was about Jews, I would be looking for my passport.'[56] In addition, Blair's growing emotional and political affiliation with the hard Right could be seen not just in his friendships with Bush, Aznar, Berlusconi and Sarkozy, but also in his decision to give wholesale, uncritical support for Israel in its 2006 invasion of Lebanon – a war that was opposed by the majority of Britons. Labour's poll ratings fell to the low thirties for the first time since 1992, while the Conservatives under Cameron had seemingly rebuilt their base to gain the support of about 36 per cent of the voting public.

Blair, who had thus far survived the unprecedented opposition to his decision to invade Iraq, was spared embarrassment at conference over the matter, and suffered no serious parliamentary moves against him through the ensuing years of chaos. Robin Cook, the only anti-war MP with sufficient clout to have a chance of competing for the leadership, died in the summer of 2005. So it was that when conditions finally ripened for Blair's departure, the avowed causes of his ousting were as depoliticised as could be. In 2006, a letter sent by some of the 2001 intake of Labour MPs to Blair suggested that he had been 'an exceptional Labour Prime Minister', but that without a change in the leadership it was 'less likely that we will win the next election'. Tom Watson's resignation letter affirmed the same idea: 'Your leadership has been visionary and remarkable. The party and nation owes you an incalculable debt.' But for the sake of Labour being 're-elected at the next general election', it was time for him to stand down.[57]

Not a single policy or decision of the old regime was criticised by the coup plotters – which was just as well since the man behind the coup, Gordon Brown, was as up to his neck in it as Blair. The turf war between the Blair and Brown factions of New Labour, notwithstanding the vain attempts by pundits and politicians to find an issue of principle between them, seems to have been chiefly about who should lead the project. Brown's oscillation between Hamlet-like procrastination and furious private rages directed at New Labour's co-founder, was a drama without the slightest wider resonance: Brown simply thought that he should inherit the project without debate and without any challenger. And, having worked out a compromise with Blair on the timing of his exit, he was duly inaugurated without any election process, as Labour MPs prevented possible rivals, such as John McDonnell, from even getting on the ballot. Brown's leadership was welcomed with a deep sigh of relief by some ministers, but the relief barely lasted a year. The disillusionment of New Labour apparatchiks with Brown was once more not over any matter of political substance, but had to do with a combination of personal loyalties, ambitions and Brown's apparent strategic blunders. In particular, having failed to call a snap election in 2007, he had seen Labour's poll ratings decline and walked into a major global economic crisis for which Labour had to take responsibility and over which it had limited time to manage. Straw, who had rallied for Brown, later declared that he would have been a better prime minister.[58]

The looming problems with the global economy had not been totally invisible. As early as September 2007, Northern Rock – one of the UK's subprime mortgage lenders – began to appeal to the Bank of England for liquidity support. The sectoral imbalances in the British economy, the weakness of its manufacturing base, pitiful levels of research & development, the ongoing slump in productivity only made up for by long working hours and an expanded workforce, and the housing bubble, had all been apparent for some considerable time before then.[59] All of this, above all the centrality of debt and speculation to the British economic model, made the UK particularly susceptible to the credit crunch when it struck. While the Conservatives are opportunistic in claiming that the economic mess was one made by Labour, their mendacity should not be allowed to obscure the extent to which New Labour created a British haven for banks and speculators.[60] As the crisis struck, Brown's position was suddenly elevated and dignified, whereas it had been increasingly frustrated and diminished beforehand. Having developed his relationships with Washington and Wall Street power-brokers since those hesternal days of the early 1990s, and taken a leading role in negotiating Britain's integration into the Washington Consensus, he was well-placed to take part in the globally orchestrated interventions to prevent a banking collapse and sustain economic demand – a role for which he gained considerable political credit with the electorate. The net effect of these interventions was to heighten the power of the banks: in effect, it was not so much that failing banks were nationalised, as that the Treasury was semi-privatised and put at the disposal of the City.[61] They were to be followed by years of bracing austerity to cover the costs of bailing out the banks, while the underlying financial infrastructure was left more or less intact.[62] Brown at least signalled a mild shift from the New Labour era by raising the top rate of tax for the first time, and declaring the era of fully free markets over. But the phrase 'too little, too late' was rarely more apt: Labour crashed in the 2010 general election, with 29 per cent of the vote, the lowest share it had received since 1918.

As the New Labour project teetered on the brink of collapse, there was one group of people on whom it had made a great impression: the Tory modernisers. *Times* columnist and later Tory minister Michael Gove was one such, who expostulated, 'I can't hold it back any more – I love Tony.' The Cameron wing of the Conservative party into which Gove was inducted became enraptured by Blair, with George Osborne declaring him 'the master'.[63] This Tory faction, having taken the leadership of their party from a recalcitrantly right-wing base, had begun to slowly assimilate Blair's presentational and political lessons. In particular, Cameron had begun to triangulate New Labour on key issues, and even to outflank them to the left on some issues and some local campaigns – for example over Post Office closures or immigration. Initially, he refused to contest Labour on public spending totals, and instead focused on priorities.[64] The volte-face following the banking bailout was a mark of skilled political opportunism but, even as the Tories attacked Labour spending and began to lay the narrative demand for austerity, they were preparing to implement cuts with a 'progressive' facade.

Conclusion: The Miliband Interregnum

For the Blairites who had been plotting to get rid of Brown as soon as he took the leadership, the 2010 Labour leadership election campaign ought to have been their moment of delicious revenge. With a youthful and, by their standards,

charismatic candidate in David Miliband, they were confident of victory. But instead, the leadership was taken by
the younger, more neurotic Ed Miliband, who gained the
support of trade unionists by cautiously letting it be known
that he was slightly to the left of his brother, and would be
more receptive to the concerns of trade unionists if he won.
'Red Ed' was always a tabloid conceit, but Miliband was at
least someone who recognised the need to decisively close
the New Labour era, recover lost working-class votes,
and ever-so-slightly push at the boundaries of acceptable
neoliberal discourse. What is more, he seemed to begin
to attract new members, cautiously optimistic about the
possibility of pushing Labour moderately to the left.

Why, then, was the period of Ed Miliband's leadership
one of general fug and confusion for Labour? In part, the
answer is organisational. While Miliband's major allies
were on the soft-left of the party, he was beset on all sides
by powerfully positioned Blairites who were outraged that
their candidate had been pipped to the post. Miliband was
desperate to keep this faction onboard due in part to their
entrenched power and their potential to wreak havoc for
him. Another part of the answer is societal. The immediate response of British society to the credit crunch and
ensuing recession was to freeze, as though caught in the
headlights. It was not until late 2010 that the first glimmer
of any kind of organised revolt against austerity began to
make itself visible in the form of the students' rebellion.
And that movement, while culturally very significant and
probably laying some groundwork for a general turn to
the left among the young, was as short-lived as subsequent

public sector pensions campaigns, and the UK's miserably diminished version of the Occupy movement. As such, there was no continuous or generalised shift to the left, and in fact much of the movement after 2011 was to the racist and authoritarian right. But the most important answer was political. It was an integral part of Ed Miliband's strategy for reviving and rebranding Labour that it should seek a new synthesis of left and right, rather than be seen to move to the left. This was arguably another reason that Miliband needed the Blairites, to counter pressure from trade unionists and constituency activists to move further left than he wished to go.

The 'Blue Labour' shenanigans of the Miliband era can be interpreted in part as an attempt to anchor the response to Labour's problems to the right, with a series of appeals based on 'faith, flag and family'. In essence, while the Blairites wanted to woo middle-class Tory voters, Blue Labour wanted to flatter working-class voters drifting to the nationalist right. To achieve this, they argued, Labour had to fashion a patriotism that would attract such voters,[65] one that reversed the Left's supposed softness on crime, its indifference to the 'culture of entitlement' on welfare, and its failure to understand anger about immigration. As Blue Labour doyen Maurice Glasman put it, he wanted Labour to be somewhere that members of the far Right rabble, the English Defence League, might feel at home.[66] This was quite at odds with the view of Blairite insider Dan Hodges, who described how the party leadership had attempted to 'ape the language of the BNP' only to succeed in 'boosting the BNP'[67] by driving their obsessions up the political agenda. It also gave Cameron, who was not averse to using a 'muscular' rhetoric on immigration when it suited him, the opportunity to deride Labour's 'Alf Garnett' race politics.[68] Miliband nonetheless cleaved hard to this strategy throughout his reign.

The rightward tilt was not just a question of Labour seeking to co-opt anti-immigrant rhetoric for the centre-Left. Soon, while Shadow Chancellor Ed Balls relinquished his brief flirtation with anti-austerity economics, Miliband was adopting a more rigorously punitive version of welfare policy than his New Labour predecessors had managed, at least at the level of policy. In addition to a welfare cap, Miliband proposed that those who had not worked in the previous five years should have their benefits cut, retirement ages should rise and parents should be forced into work-related training as soon as their child hit the age of three.[69] This was all laid out by Shadow Work and Pensions Secretary Liam Byrne, someone on the right of the New Labour project with a flair for pugnacious populism – his election campaign, managed by seasoned right-winger Tom Watson, had pledged to 'smash teen gangs' and stop benefits for 'failed asylum seekers'. And indeed, as pernicious as the policy was the rhetoric, which was culpably aligned with that of the populist Right – just as Labour sought to (gently) bash the bankers and call for 'responsible capitalism', so it sought to (harshly) incriminate the poorest as yet another usurping pressure on the 'squeezed middle'.[70]

The British nationalism that Miliband sought to mobilise had another purpose, however. One of the reasons that New Labour had so fanatically pursued its 'Britishness' agenda was to ward off the menace of Scottish independence. The devolved institutions that New Labour had itself created, the better to forestall such questions, had become a terrain in which the SNP consistently outmanoeuvred and out-classed their Labour rivals. By 2011, the SNP, having simply demonstrated a better ability than Labour to defend basic social-democratic rights such as free higher education, had swept the elections at Holyrood with a landslide. By the following year, they had gained an agreement with Cameron that there would be a referendum on independence come 2014. Since the Tories had little in the way of a base or party machine to fight the campaign in Scotland, they left it to the Scottish Labour Party, the bastion of the Labour Right, to take the lead. It was, of course, not compulsory for Labour to wage this fight and, having decided to do so, it did not have to form an open alliance with the Tories. In so doing, Labour merely underlined the extent to which there was a policy consensus at Westminster on essential matters from Trident to spending cuts. While the pro-independence campaign highlighted that Scotland need never again have a Conservative Government like the one which at that moment was privatising the NHS, Labour showed that within the Union, there would be a Tory Government whoever was in office. This not only fatally alienated much of its core vote – with the 'No' vote being concentrated in working-class heartlands like Glasgow – it also set itself up for perverse attacks from the Conservatives for supposed 'softness' on the SNP.

Miliband had always been so terrified of being thought of as in any sense left-wing. He capped his first year as leader by assuring the *Sun* that 'Red Ed Is Dead',[71] while posing with a copy of said paper. Later, when Emily Thornberry posted an apparently disobliging photograph of a St George's Cross-strewn house in Rochester, Miliband forced her resignation so that no one would think he lacked 'respect' for such patriotism.[72] Whenever the shade of 'Red Ed' seemed on the brink of resurfacing, Miliband took pains to ward it off by clumsily veering to the right. The Conservatives duly took this as a sign of weakness on Miliband's part and, despite Labour's self-destructive leadership of the 'Better Together' campaign, they embarked on a campaign to preempt any potential Labour–SNP coalition after the election by depicting Miliband as Alex Salmond's puppet. Miliband took fright, and used every available platform to attack the SNP, particularly on the two policies on which it had strongest support: Trident, and austerity.[73] It was both tactically preposterous, since Labour had no idea what sort of *quid pro quos* it may have to engage in after an election, and unconvincing, since the demonstrative attacks were plainly bluster under fire.

Labour went into the 2015 general election faced with the defeat it had been preparing for through the last five years. The hallmarks of its campaign were the farcical 'pink bus' campaign seeking to mobilise female voters – because, apparently, women won't communicate in any other colour – and the 'Edstone' listing Labour's pledges, a fittingly terminal punctuation for a campaign that was dead on arrival. The share of the vote received by both Labour and the Conservatives barely altered: only the distribution of seats changed, as a freshly detoxified Conservative Party took advantage of the Liberal collapse to mop up their seats. This was not, *pace* the Blairites, because Miliband was too much the left-wing firebrand, or because, as Blair predictably claimed, New Labour had been ditched.[74] The Beckett review into the party's electoral failure noted that the left-wing policies were in fact among the popular things about Miliband's Labour.[75] What hamstrung Miliband was that he was invested in the worst legacies of New Labour. These included not just the ill-fated attempt to triangulate the hard Right on race and immigration, the pandering to anti-welfare resentment and the defensive British nationalism, but also Miliband's own control-freakery, his excessively presidential manner of running the party, and his determination to bring US-style campaigning methods into Britain.[76] As a party, Labour seemed to have no coherent purpose: were they out to tame capitalism, as Miliband sometimes claimed, or out to tame welfare? Were they for or against austerity? They had many populist policies which were not difficult to sell by themselves, but these often cut against the grain of the overall policy framework. As an opposition, Labour could barely bring itself to oppose – to the extent that Ed Balls openly declared before the general election that he wouldn't reverse anything from Osborne's latest budget.[77] As tacticians, they couldn't bring themselves to act intelligently, because their strategy was too invested in a way of doing politics that was bringing about Labour's destruction. This was not anti-Blairite Leftism. It was a timorous attempt to reformulate Blairism for a post-credit crunch terrain. New Labour was not dead; it was undead.

5
Prospects: Can Corbyn Win?

The Uses of Defeat

In 1861, as the American Civil War raged, the anti-slavery liberal Charles Eliot Norton wrote in praise of defeat.[1] The Union Army had suffered a bitter setback in the first battle of Bull Run, near Washington DC, its slow and ponderous action allowing an easy victory to the Confederates. The defeat was 'in no true sense a disaster', Norton wrote, and was indeed both deserved and a valuable lesson. Indeed, its 'ultimate consequences' were 'better than those of a victory would have been'. The latter would have rewarded and entrenched complacency and bad strategy, whereas defeat allowed for fast rethinking and regroupment.

Defeat is an inevitable but underrated experience in political life. It is understandable that on the political Left, at least, the scarring experiences of defeat in the 1980s – of the miners and the wider trade union movement, of Militant, of the Greater London Council, of the Labour Left – led to a weary cynicism about the possibilities for change in such a reactionary country. This deadly onslaught by the Right has been used as a primary argument in favour of the ascendancy, within the Labour Party, of a managerial caste hostile to many of its traditions – not just those associated with the Left, but even the old Right defined by the likes of Wilson, Jenkins and Callaghan.

Indeed, if principle only leads to defeat, why not turn to electoral professionals, media operators and brutal party managers with at least the virtue of a killer instinct? If nothing else avails, why not at least get some form of electoral revenge on the authors of said defeat by trusting everything to those who seem to know how to win? And if the Conservative-aligned media is so grossly powerful, why not hand the reins to those who can play the media's game? Surely those who, in such circumstances, cleave to doctrine at the expense of exercising power, even if only to mildly temper the excesses of capitalism, are at best political Don Quixotes, and at worst fanatical wreckers? Such is the essential argument of the Blairites, whose project is about making Labour an effective 'party of government' rather than an effective opposition. Forget the policy wonkery, the 'blue-sky thinking', the Geoff Mulgans and Charles Leadbeaters, the Spads and fads, and the passing manias of New Labour triviology. The celebrated cerebral spine of the Blairites was in fact flimsy because it was inessential given the paucity of ambition: it requires little intellectual finesse to leave things more or less as they are. The core of New Labour was its appeal to power. It offered a tempting thrill of success to those who had been so brutally defeated, even if the condition of that success was pre-emptive surrender on all essential questions.

And for some time, at least, the Blairites had everything their way. Through good report and ill, through privatisation, war and growing inequality, through the tumescence of a billionaire class, the NHS crisis caused by usurious Private Finance Initiatives, and the bankers' pillage, there was barely a simmering reflex of revolt in the Labour Party. Members voted with their feet, becoming inactive or resigning, while voters began to boycott the polls in unprecedented numbers. As if the whole idea of fighting for a party that had become so symbiotically dependent upon the banks, business, the media and the less liberal wings of the state was so crushingly dispiriting, so lacking in promise, that millions simply gave up. The brief frisson of victory, the beautiful summer of 1997, when all that mattered was whether you were 'up for Portillo', seemed to have given way to a post-democratic melancholia and a defeat more insidious and disabling than any which Thatcher had inflicted. In 1997, all roads had led to the 'free market'. By 2010, all roads led to austerity. Blyth Valley MP Ronnie Campbell suggested that the major difference between Labour and the Tories was that Labour would 'cut your throat slowly', while the Tories would 'cut your head off'.[2] Given such a choice, approximately 5 million voters who had supported Labour in 2010 – most of them working class – abandoned the party, largely abstaining. Nothing, not even Ed Miliband's neurotic charm, not even the frantic proliferation of new syntheses – 'Blue Labour', 'One Nation Labour', etc. – seemed able to reverse the decline.

Given this dreary history, the temptation among Corbyn's supporters might be to accentuate the positive in his leadership, form wildly unrealistic expectations, and forget about the disabling underlying weaknesses that characterise the British Left. But if defeat is a very real possibility, given the overwhelming arrangement of forces against Corbyn, it is essential to be able to learn from it and rebound. One reason that New Labour was able to thrive in the first instance was that the wrong lessons were drawn from past defeats. It was all too easy to focus on the failures of the hard-Left – which, undoubtedly, were real – but the labour movement's impasse was far more deeply structured by the dominant variations of Labourism, the main form that working-class politics had taken for most of the century. How much did the Labour Party foster or constrain the potential of the movements and social forces it sought to represent? How much did post-war social democracy contribute to their de-radicalisation? How might things have been different? While such questions were not exactly ignored, the force of the argument was usually directed against those who, for all their faults, were trying to take the Labour Party away from a repetition of the Wilson/Callaghan debacles. On the other hand, if Labour had not been defeated in 2010 and 2015, the necessary reappraisal of its limits and failures would have been postponed much further, and the sources of its degeneration would have continued unnoticed. Now that they have been noticed, it would be a mistake to submerge them behind yet more positive thinking. The point is that there is the likelihood of more educational defeats, and – if these are not to be utterly demoralising, leaving activists burned out and in a state of bewilderment – Corbyn's supporters need to position themselves where they can anticipate and act appropriately on the sources of those defeats.

What Would It Mean for Jeremy Corbyn to Succeed?

Jeremy Corbyn is in a peculiar situation. As leader of the Labour Party, he appears to enjoy the support of the great majority of the party's membership. After months of 'Project Fear', YouGov found that 66 per cent of the party's members think he's doing a good job, an increase on previous polls.[3] If he hasn't been able to construct the sort of shadow cabinet he would ideally like, he was able to appoint John McDonnell as shadow chancellor so that the overall direction of policy on austerity, welfare and public services would be left-wing. And, following a reshuffle, he was able to draft the anti-Trident MP Emily Thornberry to the Defence post, to counteract Labour's traditional bipartisanship on defence policy. He has been able to humanise Labour's policy on refugees and immigration – his first gesture as leader, characteristically, was to attend a pro-refugee rally in central London – push mental health up the agenda, commit Labour to repealing the Conservatives' anti-union laws, and contribute to George Osborne's humiliation on working families' tax credits. He has made Labour look much more like an opposition than it did before. And as Osbornite austerity deepens and affects far more households than the Conservatives were able to alienate in their first term,[4] Labour is no longer compromised by feeble attempts to triangulate the government on spending cuts.

Yet for all that, his position is extremely tenuous. Fearmongering to one side, Labour's share of the vote under Corbyn has not crashed – but it has also barely nudged above the 30 per cent mark. And however unfair it may be to blame his leadership entirely for that situation, there are sections of the parliamentary party for whom poor polling is enough to demand his head. Much of his shadow cabinet includes people quietly waiting for him to be forced to resign, while backbenchers maintain a fairly constant drumbeat of attacks. With some exceptions, media outlets and professionals overwhelmingly empathise with and support Corbyn's opponents, who are given ample air time, column inches, and praise for what they do. The majority of his supporters in the party lack the organisation, experience, visibility and power that his opponents have. Meanwhile, the wider left and labour movements from which he might draw strength are weaker than they have been for generations. It is not apparent that even if Corbyn were to win an election, he would be able to implement his core policies, which require a minimum of cooperation from business and even the financial sector. Even if Corbyn could persuade business that it doesn't stand to lose from his policies of mild redistribution, and even if he doesn't raise taxes on profits, the growth formula predicated on popping the speculative housing bubble and shifting investment toward high-technology industries is a direct challenge to the dominance of finance. The City would seek to punish such a challenge swiftly and thoroughly, such that the early days of a Corbyn administration could be expected to face currency attacks, investment strikes and downgrading by ratings agencies.

Not for the first time in recent years, the Left has been propelled to a position of influence well beyond its social and political strength, chiefly because of the etiolation of the old guard and the paucity of their analyses of – let alone solutions to – the crisis. But it is rare to catch the establishment with its pants down in this fashion, and they do tend to recover. If the opportunity is not exploited quickly to produce lasting gains, it will not be repeated soon. Thus far, 'Project Fear' has not been successful, but unless Corbyn has begun to significantly change the way Labour does politics, alter the balance of power within it, spell out a more or less coherent alternative to what might be termed the 'Osbrown consensus' and expand Labour's constituency within two or three years, he will not get another chance. So what would success look like?

Nothing raises the heckles of Labour's 'moderates' more than the idea that they should be reduced to an oppositional rump, a party of activists and street protesters, exerting influence but wielding no power. This raises the question of what sort of power it is that they think they can wield. The history of Labour governments is not such that it inspires one with a sense of their awesome puissance. Rather, one tends to find a scenario much more consistent with Perry Anderson's description:

When a Labour Government is in office, it is an isolated, spotlit enclave, surrounded on almost every side by hostile territory, unceasingly shelled by industry, press and orchestrated 'public opinion'. Each time in the end it has been overrun.[5]

Of course, no Labour government was as successful as New Labour in shaping public opinion, winning over the right-wing press barons, coalescing with industry and turning hostile territory into *terra familia*. Even that government was not spared its crises, from the Iraq War to the NHS fiscal crisis to the credit crunch. But these problems were not borne of the attempt to implement reforms from the left, and by and large they did not incur the opposition of the powerful: they were the problems which arose from accepting the terrain inherited from one's opponents. If this is what is meant by exercising power, the idea seems to have lost a significant part of its meaning.

Yet the danger is that just because the conventional ways of gauging success are less important – headlines, news cycles, poll fluctuations – Corbyn's supporters might take refuge in wishful thinking. In the gaps in knowledge about what *is* important, fantasies can take hold and unrealistic hopes abound. The excitable talk about a 'new politics' may obscure the extent to which Corbyn's project is in most respects a traditional electoral one, subject to the same logic and limitations of any such project. It seems clear that we need a new way of thinking about success, and power.

One way to define success, of course, is to start from failure. The fundamental condition shaping everything that Corbyn does, or could conceivably do, is the weakness and decline of the Left and the labour movement on which Labour has traditionally pivoted its hopes. This decline is registered at the level of organisation, in falling union density and activity, in declining membership in left-wing groups, in the makeshift and transient nature of most social movements, and in the relative sparsity of left-wing publications. It is registered at the level of ideology, in the way that it has largely been unable to shape the terrain except in a reactive and defensive way. The anti-war mobilisations of the 2000s, of course, provide a striking contrast to the general retreat on other fronts. It is registered at the level of policy where, for several decades, every major shift in the dominant party system has been about shutting down options, with party elites converging on the neoliberal centre. Left-wingers have usually been excluded from government in this period, but where they have taken office they have usually administered the orthodoxy. And of course, it is registered at the level of economy and society, where inequality and competition are the rule, and collectivist and egalitarian norms have been progressively rolled back on almost every front.

From this perspective, there are several types of benchmark that could be used to think about success. The first is organisational. Those who are expecting that Labour will be transformed into an instrument of radical change, within the brief window of opportunity available to Corbyn, are likely to be disappointed. Labour has never been that type of party, and the sources of resistance to it are considerable. As it is, Corbyn's organisational goals seem to be more limited. He has sought to rebuild the membership of

the party and revitalise its degenerating or inactive constituency branches. He has also indicated that he aims to
address the grossly top-heavy distribution of power within
the party, and create more space for its left-wing activists to
organise and shape policymaking. There are few specifics
as yet, and Corbyn has emphatically ruled out deselection campaigns, but his team appears to be briefing the
party that he aims to roll back some of the power of the
National Policy Forum created by Blair, and to devolve
more policymaking power to the membership.[6] Another
central theme of Corbyn's tenure as leader thus far is
his desire to rebuild the idea of Labour as a social movement, embedded in unions and popular campaigns. Finally,
within the Labourist 'broad church' frame of reference, he
aspires to make the other wings of the party comfortable
with the idea of a left-wing leadership and to isolate the
recalcitrant Right.

The second benchmark is ideological. Corbyn won the
Labour leadership as a radical socialist, despite the fact that
even in name, socialism has been off the agenda of mainstream British politics for a couple of decades if not longer.
This presents him and his supporters with a unique opportunity to exploit the weaknesses of the neoliberal legacy,
and to begin to reverse a decades-long trajectory to the
right. Labour, notwithstanding its inherited crises, still
communicates fairly well with working-class audiences,
and shapes popular preferences and ideas as much as it represents them. Tony Blair, for example, did far more than
Margaret Thatcher to diminish support for redistribution
and turn large numbers of people against the welfare state,

precisely because he led a party that communicated with people whom Thatcher never could. Corbyn, with all the limits of his power, has some space in which to shape an alternative agenda which goes with the grain of common sense and lived experience. His objectives on the terrain of ideology are modest and three-fold. His call for a 'kinder politics' already aims to resist the illiberal drift of opinion on immigrants and welfare, wherein repressive policies are buttressed by a form of popular social sadism.[7] He also needs to persuade the public at large that British attempts to hang onto the coat-tails of American global power – through Trident and uncritical participation in its wars – are neither humanitarian nor in the interests of security. Finally, and most importantly, he needs to demonstrate that an alternative economic formula is both desirable and workable, since his commitments on welfare and the public sector depend on the growth that would result from re-tooling the economy. This is a long game: ideological territories are shaped over generations, not in time for electoral cycles.

But electoral cycles will not wait for Corbyn's long game. And his survival could depend on this third, important benchmark for his success. As one Labour member puts it,

> Being a constitutionalist party, Labour always measures itself by vote metrics. To state openly that we should put the 2020 election in the bin would be regarded in horror by all sections of the party. A loss then would be widely interpreted as a campaign fought and defeated on the grounds of socialist ideas … All this means that the only thing that could blunt the complaints of the centre and the right would be electoral success.[8]

Here, however, Labour's problems are not merely conjunctural but structural: that is, Labour doesn't just have its customary problem with affluent swing voters, it has a far more serious problem with working-class voters. This problem has deeper roots than New Labour, and a degree of class dealignment is visible in the votes for most European social-democratic parties, but the problem has radicalised in recent years. If it were to continue in the same trajectory, the term 'Pasokification'[9] would apply with force.

There is, of course, no guarantee that just because Corbyn is not an economic liberal that he can repair this damage. Just because the Blairites are wrong to blame 'left-wing' policies for losing the 2015 election, it doesn't follow that left-wing policies alone would have won it. And he certainly stands little chance of recovering Scotland in the immediate term. He has inherited a Labour Party whose share of the vote seems to be stuck at around 30 per cent, nowhere near enough to form a viable plurality. Corbyn has recognised that a big part of Labour's problem is low turnout among key, would-be Labour-supporting demographics – young people and poor voters, and seeks to rebuild the disintegrating core vote while motivating abstainers. But he also has to find a way to turn a generic anti-austerity message into an electoral offer, a programme for government, that goes well beyond the core vote.

The final benchmark is policy. This is, in some ways, the most difficult of Corbyn's tasks, because it means reckoning not only with the government, but also his own parliamentary party. Here, it doesn't help that he faces the obstruction of a wing of the party, including in his own cabinet, who have thus far instrumentalised parliamentary debates on Syria and Trident, thereby making the government's task easy, while weakening their own leadership. Nor is it particularly helpful that Labour's candidate for the mayor of London is doing everything he can, bar changing political parties, to distance himself from the leadership in the hope of flattering Tory voters in a predominantly Labour-voting city. Nonetheless, things aren't as bleak on this front as they may appear. Despite the extraordinary class-based invective of opponents such as John Mann MP – 'In the Dog and Duck, they could understand his words. Nationalise the railways. Alf and Bert could agree with that – sounds reasonable enough. Stop austerity. Samantha and Craig can smell a pay rise for themselves here'[10] – the majority of the parliamentary party seem to have accepted opposition to austerity and privatisation as their bread and butter. And, notwithstanding the dissenters and the unseemly praise lavished on Hillary Benn's mendacious pro-war speech comparing the warmongers to the republican side in the Spanish Civil War, Corbyn carried the majority of the parliamentary party with him on Syria. The rump of those actively seeking to oust Corbyn are a minority and, for the moment, reduced to ineffectual lashing out. Far more effective are those, like Deputy Leader Tom Watson, who quietly tolerate the situation and refrain from criticising Corbyn directly, yet use their influence to undermine his policies – above all on Syria and Trident. Yet Corbyn must somehow work with them to develop a plausible programme for office, one that they will actually try to implement given the opportunity.

These various ends are not necessarily mutually com-
patible. It may not be possible to reconstitute Labour as a
party with a thriving Left without paying a cost in terms
of party peace. It may not be possible to 'build the social
movement' as Corbyn seeks to do without alienating some
allies – unions have already expressed unhappiness over
his foreign policy positions, some officials preferring him
to focus on 'real life issues' of wages and spending cuts.[11]
Such a retreat to the traditional, narrow, sectional concerns
of trade unions is likely to be a mistake on their part, one
that could cut off potential sources of new recruitment and
support. But Corbyn may struggle to persuade them of
that. It may not be possible to rebuild the core vote and
simultaneously win over enough additional voters to win a
general election. It may not be possible to engage in prefer-
ence-shaping, to shift the ideological terrain, without being
willing to pay an electoral cost for a period of time. And
there will be disagreements even on the left of the Labour
Party about the order of priorities. For Labour activist and
Independent columnist Liam Young, Corbyn can achieve
'something larger than simply electoral success – he can
change the debate and importantly for us internal cam-
paigners, solidify the position of the left within the Labour
Party'. For other activists, since 'the right's chances are
completely tied to the party's electoral fortunes', Corbyn
needs to deliver a 'credible alternative vision of how else
electoral success can be delivered' even if the party needs
to be 'much less monopolised by electoralism'.[12] The point
is, however, that it is not even possible to think of these
trade-offs, to weigh up the different versions of success, if

the focus is narrowly on electoral outcomes and psepho-logical minutiae.

The Church Is Not Brick and Mortar

Christians are apt to say, 'the church is not brick and mortar'. It is, rather, made up of a community of believers. A secular way of putting this is that the party is not primar-ily its money or its bureaucracy, but its members. Insofar as Corbyn aspires to rebuild the Labour Party, his brief is to recruit active members. Already, Corbyn can claim some success in attracting tens of thousands of people to the Labour Party, thus reversing the almost universal trend in party politics in Britain and across most industrial democ-racies for some decades. Jeremy Corbyn's grass-roots supporters, the potential missionaries of twenty-first-century socialism, are disproportionately young and working class. As Freddie Sayers of YouGov put it in the *Guardian*,

Corbynmania was a youth movement and a social media move-ment, but it was also a working-class movement. As a group, the Labour 'selectorate' that voted in the leadership election were more educated and well-to-do than the population at large, but within that the most 'normal' group were actually Corbyn supporters. Only 26 per cent of Corbyn supporters had a household income of more than £40,000, slightly less than the national figure of 27 per cent. (Andy Burnham, Yvette Cooper and Liz Kendall supporters were progressively better off at 29, 32 and 44 per cent respectively.) So Corbyn got the cool kids and the working-class leftwing.[13]

They are, in short, exactly the sorts of voters whom Labour has been losing hand over fist. This is the problem the Corbynistas face. The Labour Party has not suddenly become a democratic organisation just because they got their man elected. The power has not shifted to the grass roots. It is still with the party machine, and a largely right-wing parliamentary group. The institutions of Labour are ranged against Corbyn and his supporters, and they are backed up by their connections to the state, the media, think tanks and businesses. Nor, for that matter, has parliament become more democratic overnight. The same imperviousness to popular pressure that has enabled successive governments to implement unpopular privatisations and pursue unpopular wars persists today. The establishment is ancient, deeply entrenched, recalcitrant and difficult to shift. And the political class that has emerged from the Thatcher era is callous, indifferent to popular will and determined to cling on to power. The mere fact of having members, therefore, is not enough. The efficacy of those members depends on how they are organised. And here not all signs are good. Margaret Corvid, a Labour member in Plymouth, notes with exasperation that even while most members cleave to the traditional goal of a Labour government, with Corbyn becoming prime minister, 'ironically, most of the people wanting this, and clamouring for it, are not doing a lot of the work that will make that happen, like knocking on doors. So, you have low engagement, you have only a handful of people getting involved'.[14]

In an effort to capitalise on the energy of Labour's ranks of new, radical members, some of Jeremy Corbyn's supporters set up the campaigning group Momentum. The idea was positive: members who had mobilised in the heat of a campaign should not just be ignored and left to their own devices once the election was concluded. While Labour has never been a socialist party and is unlikely to become one, activists can at least create a durable space for themselves. Yet it has produced a chorus of condemnation from the Labour Right and their allies in the media for its supposed bullying of Labour MPs. Even Deputy Leader Watson, a seasoned and nuanced warrior of the Labour Right who tends to pick his fights carefully, denounced it as 'a rabble'.[15]

In truth, there is little evidence for this, and it is not absolutely clear what Momentum will become. The group has encouraged members to participate in classic forms of street activism and protest, but it has also sought to make advances on Labour's internal bodies – with some modest success thus far. It could be a genuinely democratic grass-roots movement, or a left-wing equivalent of pressure groups such as the New Labour-backing Progress and the soft-left Compass, or a machinery for the furthering of the influence of seasoned hard-left operators in Labour's committees. As with any such fragile new organisation, it is betraying a propensity to attract various groupuscules, factions and office-seekers, which could end quite badly. If members of proscribed groups decide to join Labour in order to work within Momentum, they could hand the party machine an opportunity to disrupt its efforts by using the Compliance Unit to purge the interlopers. Irrespective of the fairness of such proscriptions, misguided entryism merely legitimises such crackdowns and makes life harder for Labour activists.[16] Some members also complain of the excessive dominance within the group of factions like the Livingstone-aligned Socialist Alternative, or specific individuals. It is difficult to parse these claims, which others members dismiss as paranoia or a right-wing hobby horse, but it would be a shame if the first steps in organising a fragile new Left were to be bogged down in the minutiae of individual careers, jockeying for influence and the backward tendencies of Britain's old, exhausted, fractal Left.

What is more, many of the newer members are as yet ideologically unformed and politically indeterminate, while the older Bennite and Militant-style leftovers are, in general, too ideologically formed and too politically inflexible to be effective. Frenzied stories about Trots taking over branch meetings aside, the new Labour Left is more potential than reality, its organisation is nascent, and it is roughly divided between those who lack experience and those whose experience is one of trauma. The cultural schism between those who still sing the Red Flag at parties, and those who emerged from the more modern-day milieux of Climate Camp, the student movement and Occupy, is a palpable obstacle. The younger are more culturally fluent, know how to use Twitter, aren't obsessed with setting up street stalls on a Saturday morning, and are capable of expressing the Left's arguments in an idiom that is accessible – but they do not, as yet, have the confidence to lead. It is also not yet clear what kind of party they will want Labour to be, how they want it to relate to the wider organisational and social stream of the Left, or what their attitude to trade unions will be. The various left-wing groupings within Labour – be they Momentum, the Labour Representation Committee or Red Labour – are as yet underdeveloped, and hardly any match for the immense, lordly dominion of the parliamentary party and the electoral-professional caste running daily party life.

Yet perhaps the greatest challenge Labour is faced with concerns the seemingly intractable strategic dilemmas over just how radical it can be. Corbyn has disappointed his more left-wing supporters by ruling out deselections of right-wing MPs, and by calling on councils not to resist government cutbacks by setting illegal budgets. On both these points, his critics have a point. Blairites wasted no time in recomposing the parliamentary party as soon as they had power, and it could be argued that MPs who choose not to represent the policies on which Corbyn was elected leader ought to be able to explain their position to members. The foam-flecked scare stories about activists seeking a 'ruthless purge' of Labour[17] obscures this basic democratic fact. Yet, in truth, the parliamentary party has never represented the membership. And if a concerted campaign for re-selection battles were to be mounted across the party, this would run the risk of providing ballast to a right-wing sabotage campaign, and alienating potential allies. One reason why the backbench malcontents dare not act against Corbyn is precisely because they fear it would rebound horribly, end in failure and ultimately legitimise a deselection campaign. If deselection campaigns are embarked upon, however, they can potentially use this to win some of the 41 per cent of members and supporters who didn't back Corbyn for a concerted drive against the Left. By the same token, local councils which implement government cutbacks are sure to turn off and demoralise Labour voters, and a Left that is seen to acquiesce with such austerity measures could rapidly discredit itself in the eyes of the public. Yet if members were to campaign to try to force these councils to set illegal budgets in a gesture of Poplarist defiance, it seems unlikely that they would have the political muscle to succeed, or to weather the backlash if they did. And these types of dilemmas would become more acute were there to emerge significant social movements pushing further in the direction of radical change than the Labour leadership felt able to go for reasons of electoral and parliamentary arithmetic. Activists would then have to choose between maintaining discipline for the purposes of winning a Labour government – the traditional prize – or being willing to sacrifice that possibility for the chance (perhaps slim, perhaps nebulous) of winning something else. These are dilemmas, it must be emphasised, which derive from the weakness and backwardness of the Left.

What is reasonably clear is that, while activists will always have to prioritise between party-building and movement-building, between electioneering and agitating, they need a form of organisation that enables them to do this rather than one that embroils them in internecine power struggles or the minutiae of the resolutionary Left. They have only a small window in which to overcome these dilemmas and to devise a coherent strategy to build a Left that is habitable, durable and not thoroughly off-putting to those with whom it seeks to work. Absent palpable successes, they will soon begin to vote with their feet, and find other ways to be politically active. At which point, Corbyn's opponents would have the advantage.

A Gentle Push at the Boundaries of Debate

One of Corbyn's virtues is that he is not overly impressed by that reified category we call 'public opinion'. That is not to say he is indifferent to what people think – but he wants to change opinion, to lead it, rather than merely reflect it in various poll-tested triangulations. On the three main planks of the economy and public spending, foreign policy and a 'kinder politics', Corbyn's agenda is not exactly the *Communist Manifesto*. It is not even one of the more radical Labour manifestos. In all, it constitutes an attempt to gently push the boundaries of debate to the left, to open new possibilities, and to push back against some of the nastier forms of right-wing politics. Yet, even these objectives could overwhelm him.

Corbyn has a lot to work with in terms of popular discontents. There is not at present a tremendous popular enthusiasm for British wars, most people do not support Trident,[18] spending cuts and privatisation in vital services are wildly unpopular, and clear majorities have always supported renationalising the railways and utilities.[19] Meanwhile, the bankers are widely reviled,[20] taxing the rich is popular,[21] the out-of-control housing market and soaring rents are ensuring that most people in large urban areas will never become homeowners and will have to dedicate the majority of their income to rent-seekers. The majority

of people still own a home, but the rate of home ownership is declining for everyone under the age of sixty-five,
and sharply declining for everyone under the age of thirty-
five.[22] British banks and British tanks do not appear to be
doing most British people any favours.

Corbyn also has the advantage that he is able to oppose
the government far more consistently than his predecessors, something he accentuated during the leadership
campaign: 'Ed Miliband made some very good points about
zero-hours contracts, about young people's opportunities,
about poverty wages, and so on – very good stuff indeed,
but the problem was that the fundamental economic strategy of the party was a form of austerity-lite.'[23] Ceding
ground in this way was a sure route to defeat, since it both
eroded the credibility of Labour's campaign on living
standards (about which it could do little if it accepted austerity), and also de-fanged Labour in its oddly half-hearted
attempts to challenge the Tory narrative that Labour had
created the national deficit through public spending. Yet if
that was the end of it, it would be hard to explain how the
Conservatives won.

The Conservatives have been able to profit from the
shared assumption across all parties that the current economic model is the one we have to live with: there is no
alternative. With that framing assumption, it has been relatively easy to displace attention from Britain's economic
dysfunctions to Labour's supposed overspend. Corbyn's
most pressing task is to demonstrate that there is a coherent alternative economic model. Only on this basis can
he support his policies of protecting welfare and public

services. His Shadow Chancellor John McDonnell has begun the work on this with what sounds like a modern version of Harold Wilson's programme for growth based on technological innovation.[24] He has enlisted a series of high-profile economic advisors whose thinking is counter to the old neoliberal orthodoxy, and who argue that growth based on inequality, debt and leaving as much as possible to the private sector is unsustainable.[25] In particular, he borrows from Mariana Mazzucato the idea of an 'entrepreneurial state'.[26] Mazzucato's highly praised book of the same name describes how major growth vectors arise from extensive public sector investment and experimentation – the prize example being Apple's global dominion, which owes its iPod, iPhone and iPad technology to innovations first made in the state sector. McDonnell can build a case for this on the pathologies of the British economy. There are, in fact, few truly dynamic sectors, aside from the City's role as an historic hub of global finance – a status it has held on to by becoming, under Major, Blair and Brown, Wall Street's 'Guantánamo', an offshore island where normal legality doesn't apply[27] – there are only aerospace and pharmaceuticals. Osborne and the Bank of England look forward to a long period of 'export-led growth', but there is little for Britain to export since its manufacturing industries have been allowed to shrink and rust.

Even so, strictly in terms of what people believe, polling suggests that despite the myriad discontents with the British economic model, at present more people are wary of state intervention than would support it.[28] There is support for some limited regulation and intervention, and a degree of public ownership, but the majority of people, having lived for years with the assumption that state intervention cannot work, remain to be convinced that a more sustained interventionist thrust is called for.[29] It is not that there is anything inherently unelectable about some forms of economic Leftism. Even so moderate a figure as Canada's Justin Trudeau managed to reverse the fortunes of his Liberal Party and get elected on a mildly anti-austerity programme explicitly committed to raising the deficit for three years to fund stimulus spending. It is just that Corbyn and McDonnell have to begin to shape and lead opinion for the ends of progress in a way that Labour leaders haven't done for some time. There are some encouraging signs on this front, insofar as McDonnell is promoting a series of public meetings supporting the 'new economics' while Labour activists are holding local events educating activists on economics.[30] It is as yet too early to gauge their impact, but the weight of received opinion and ingrained assumptions that they are working against should not be underestimated.

What is more, Corbyn will need to demonstrate that within that framework the welfare state is a crucial support to popular living standards, can be responsive to contemporary needs, and need not necessarily be a zone for zero-sum competition over scarce resources. Ipsos Mori's 'Generations' poll demonstrates a fairly consistent trajectory of decline in support for the welfare state.[31] This is no doubt in part due to the decline in support for welfare among the dominant parties. Labour's pathetic abstention in the vote on the government's welfare bill underlined the extent to which a parliamentary consensus has developed that the social wage, the benefits that many of Labour's constituents depend upon, must be pared back. But it is also because a majority of people have been persuaded of claims about the welfare system that have no basis in fact[32] – for example, that welfare payments are much higher than they really are, or that immigrants receive a far greater share of welfare spending than is actually the case. One of the saddest facts about contemporary Britain is the susceptibility of many people to a kind of resentful social sadism on this issue – it is notable, for instance, that of the policies in Osborne's first budget after the 2015 election, among the most popular were measures which only benefited the well-off, such as raising the threshold of inheritance tax; or those which only harmed the poorest, such as lowering the benefit cap and cutting housing benefits for the under-twenty-ones.[33] The fact that this is so indicates something about how, in part due to New Labour's influence, people view the economy as a place not only of 'efficiency' but also of 'merit'. That is, Osborne has been able to mobilise long-ingrained popular assumptions that to be deserving is to be in work, that those who don't work or need benefits are an unproductive burden enfeebled by welfare dependency, and that nothing would be better for their souls than the whip of market discipline.

This is merely to give a taste of the ideological difficulties that Corbyn's project faces. It is not unthinkable that Corbyn could, given a new economic crisis and a continued decline in living standards, find a way to articulate popular discontents within a relatively simplified narrative about how things got so bad, who is to blame and what is to be done. One thinks here of Bernie Sanders constantly hammering 'the billionaire class', Syriza lambasting the 'troika', and Podemos denouncing 'la casta' to great effect. However, it is striking that, thus far, Corbyn has pointedly refused to identify a class opponent in this way, instead sticking to the conventional Labour *modus operandi* of attacking 'the Tories'. This reticence in articulating a class division may be motivated by a prudent desire not to alienate possible business allies, or it may flow ineluctably from his 'politics of kindness' which seems to foreswear such rousing populism. Whatever the reason, such circumspection could prove to be a disabling limitation in an era when class polarisation often proves more important to voting outcomes than traditional party affiliation.

Perhaps part of the problem may be that ideological battles tend to yield their fruit in the long term. If Sanders is able to turn fire against 'the billionaire class' in a way that no Democratic candidate has before, it is because he is working on elements of popular ideology that have long been in development. Ideological battles don't offer immediate rewards, but they shape the terrain on which future political conflicts are settled. And outside of stagey confrontations in parliament or on news programmes, the battles that matter are largely taking place beneath the radar, in direct, regular contact with people. Corbyn, had he not been given the responsibility of leading a broad party within such a short space of time, might have felt more able to experiment and push at the boundaries of acceptable discourse. But now he is necessarily compromised in waging this battle by the necessity of finding intelligent mediations between what is desirable, what is electorally feasible, what his parliamentary party will tolerate and what can realistically be implemented in government.

This suggests that there will need to be a division of labour wherein his grass-roots support must continually push the agenda farther than he is able to. They are, in fact, best placed to conduct this struggle, since winning ideological gains is not just about 'the battle of ideas'. Ideology is about where those ideas connect with lived experience, and that connection is not formed by manifestos and leaflets alone, far less than by savvy public relations strategies which are necessarily limited by having to work with the assumptions ingrained within sections of the media. Ideology in this sense is close to what Raymond Williams meant by 'culture', when he argued that 'culture is ordinary'.[34] It is what people take for granted in their everyday practice, the basic axioms they live by and which shape their tastes, their sense of justice and fairness, as well as their sense of the possible. It is also the beliefs, conscious or otherwise, which they take pleasure in, cherish and are passionately committed to. One reason why it simply isn't good enough to 'win the battle of ideas' is precisely that people take far too much pleasure in their beliefs to give them up for a well-articulated policy statement.

Conceived in these terms, the battle to win ideological space is clearly not something that can be separated from the necessity of grassroots political organisation. It is not possible to shift people's beliefs and assumptions without regularly spending time with them. Nor is it possible to win volunteers, recruits, converts, the sorts of people who will proselytise and keep the faith through good and ill, without at least talking to them, and ideally doing something along-side them. It is therefore to his advantage that Corbyn seems to recognise his role as an enabler and organiser, someone who can make space for people to do things that he cannot.

Electability

Even in what is increasingly a post-democracy, elections matter. And in a normal political situation, Jeremy Corbyn shouldn't be electable. The common sense of the media and the political class should prevail. And there are reasons to suppose that Corbyn's critics have a point. He polls poorly, thus far unable to expand Labour's base beyond the approximately 30 per cent support that it has had since the 2015 election.[35] He leads Labour against a centre-seeking Conservative Party that has been detoxified by the Liberals and – even as it wields the axe – is subtle enough to encroach on Labour's thematics, whether on the 'living wage' or on who really represents the workers. He leads a party that is now widely held to be responsible for the 2008 financial crisis, a theme that was repeated *ad nauseum* by both parties of the coalition government. As a radical socialist, his views are those of a significant minority of the public, but not of an electorally viable plurality. As an anti-war Leftist in a country that hasn't really ever come to terms with the loss of the empire, he is easy to vilify as a threat to 'national security' in a way that has not been possible with more conventional overseas equivalents such as Bernie Sanders. On Defence policy, too, the Tories have lost no time in hammering away at the panic button. Scotland is likely to be lost to Labour for the foreseeable future: Corbyn's efforts to outflank the SNP from the left are having no impact, as most voters see them as being 'indistinguishable from the Tories'.[36] Corbyn is surrounded on his own benches, front and back, by those who range from sceptics to outright saboteurs who now want Labour to lose and who are determined to see the leader hamstrung through a daily series of confected scandals. And while he is popular among Labour's grass roots, the power in the party is still vested in the machine.

What might happen, though, if we work with a different proposition? Suppose this isn't a normal political situation, Corbyn's leadership victory wasn't a fluke and the old metrics of success don't hold? What happens if we conceptualise all of the supposed reasons why Corbyn should not be electable in a slightly different way? Labour polls poorly under Corbyn, but no worse than before he was elected. Part of the reason for its current poor polling is the post-election adjustment made by polling companies, who now weight against younger and poorer voters. Yet part of Corbyn's brief is to persuade those voters to turn out in mass. He is confronting a centre-seeking party at a time when the centre is not necessarily as broad as it has been, when living standards continue to decline and parts of the middle class that were dependent on the public sector are declining. As leader, he is also far less incriminated by past Labour performance and perceived failings than any of his rivals would have been – above all the credit crunch, which most voters blame Labour for, and which was decisive in losing Labour two consecutive elections.[37] As a socialist, he must win over and lead people who are not socialists – but it is the task of virtually every political leader, of the left, right and centre, to assemble coalitions. Blair did not win office because most of his voters agreed with his politics, but because he persuaded most of them that he was the best deal they were going to get. It is surely not beyond Corbyn to make a more tempting offer than that.

Corbyn's views on war and Trident tend to be closer to the balance of public opinion than his rivals like to pretend, while 'national security' panics aren't as effectual as they might have been in a Cold War world. Scotland will not return to Labour, but Scotland has rarely in electoral history been key to Labour winning office. And if a coalition with the SNP should prove necessary, Corbyn's stance on Trident and austerity would be an asset. Finally, while there are those in Labour who would like to sabotage the leadership, and who are endlessly extolled by the media, it is notable that on the most contentious recent issue that Corbyn has faced in the parliamentary party – the vote on bombing Syria – he carried with him most of his MPs and even a majority of the shadow cabinet. He has the very vocal support of Labour big hitters such as John Prescott and Len McCluskey. The minority who are ceaselessly agitating for a party coup are likely, through their bombastic, deluded air of righteous victimhood and smug sense of entitlement, to powerfully alienate those whom they would need as supporters and allies. On the other hand, with the overwhelming support of the party grass roots, Corbyn could presumably lead a process of democratic reform in the Labour Party, which would put manners on the party's fixers.

The problem is this. The Labour Right, though unimaginative and timid even in terms of achieving their own limited objectives, are correct to identify the problem that the number of voters who support Corbyn-style socialism are by themselves too few to win an election. The metropolitan Left based in large urban centres and university towns may be a sufficient source of activists to drive a movement for change. The educated precariat, who are politicised and have some time and resources, could take a leading role, insofar as there is a movement for them to lead. And surrounding them are some social groups who never particularly cared for neoliberalism but were previously silenced because they lacked representation. But beyond that, there are far more provincial areas where the concerns of the urban working class are not as visible, where the difficulties with home ownership and renting are not as acute, where there is a sense of neglect and distance from Westminster, but where social attitudes tend to be less progressive. Among these constituencies, it is even quite possible that having a leadership represent a politically correct metropolitan constituency would be just as alienating as a leadership that represented economic liberalism.

The results of elections held thus far are not sufficient to make any definitive judgement one way or the other about how well Corbyn is able to bridge the gap. However, the signals from opinion polling and scattered local election results are not good. Labour's poll ratings in the first eight months since the 2015 general election were on average eight points behind those of the Conservatives – the worst performance by Labour after a general election since the Second World War.[38] This isn't Corbyn's fault, since Labour was in a mess when he took the leadership, but he has not yet been able to reverse the trends. While he has probably not impeded the reconstruction of Labour's core vote, and has probably accelerated it, the evidence is that it has been on the mend since the 2010 defeat. The increased vote for Labour in Oldham West under Corbyn is not as big as the improvements Labour experienced in previous by-elections during the Miliband interregnum. Elsewhere, the polls indicate a generally poor Labour vote.[39] Meanwhile in London, the heartland of the metropolitan Left, where Corbyn's support is strongest, he will be denied the opportunity to take any credit from Labour's victory by the fact that Sadiq Khan has done everything he can to distance himself from Corbyn in a bid to charm Tory voters.

This is a serious problem for Corbyn. The main point of Labour's existence is to win Labour governments, however much these governments may undermine Labour's other purposes in the long term. That is so ingrained into the party culture that Corbyn cannot be seen to challenge it. As one Labour activist put it,

> The Right's chances are completely tied to the party's electoral fortunes. … the key now is for Corbyn to bust this 'iron law' that elections can only be won from the centre, triangulating, demonstrating the leader is not 'in hock' to the unions or his core voters.

... They shouldn't obsess from week to week about polling trends. But they do need to establish a credible alternative vision of how else electoral success can be delivered.[40]

Were Corbyn to address Labour's problems frankly, however, he would admit that the two-party system has no future in British politics, and that Labour's monopoly over left-of-centre voters ended long ago. He would look for proportional representation and think about new electoral alliances. Corbyn has rightly acknowledged the need to change the constitutional settlement of the UK, and to de-centralise power while disbursing the resources to make power effective. And yet, were he to address Labour's problems in Scotland, he would have to go further still. He would be compelled to acknowledge that Labour's almost superstitious deference to the British state and its constitutional arrangements prevented it from understanding the real causes of pro-independence sentiment. He would admit that British nationalism is at least no better than Scottish nationalism, and that Labour's alliance with the Tories and the British state was a political disaster as well as a strategic one. And he would frankly state that the SNP, having won Scottish working-class voters on the strength of moderate social-democratic policies, is now closer to where Corbyn himself stands on pressing policy issues than many of his own backbenchers. In short, he would force Labour to adapt to its greatly reduced status, and think creatively about how this adjustment could be achieved beyond the usual expedient of swerving to the right in order to attract more swing voters.

It is certainly arguable that if Corbyn succeeds in his goal of mobilising poorer and younger voters, the polls will be confounded, since they are weighted on the potentially misguided assumption that these voters will not turn out. There is a generational shift taking place that has been responsible for left-wing surges in many countries, from Ecuador to Greece, and is now visible in the Corbyn and Sanders phenomena. And while it is difficult to say when these tendencies will mature, it would be complacent to assume that the 2020 electorate will be roughly the same as that which voted in 2015. If that is true, it is still uncertain how any added 'Generation Y' voters will be geographically concentrated, and whether any such possible reconfiguration might be sufficient for Labour to win a parliamentary majority. Moreover, while Sanders – if he gets the nomination – will be facing down the hard (near-fascist) Right in the shape of Ted Cruz or Donald Trump (the religious and secular far-Right incarnate), Corbyn's Labour will confront a centre-seeking Conservative Party that has successfully steered itself into former Liberal heartlands and plans on staying put. There is also still the prospect, increasingly likely, that Britain's sluggish economy will enter into another recession before the 2020 election, thus raising the salience of those discontents that Corbyn is already operating upon. Even so, as the aftermath of the credit crunch shows us, there is no guarantee that a crisis of capitalism necessarily rebounds to the benefit of the Left.

There is, however, one last factor which should make Corbyn's opponents pause: namely, the decay of the representative link. Everywhere, there are shocks, sudden surges and reversals, unpredictable and unpredicted by pundits (who have yet to display any discernible humility in their prognoses as a result). The old regime is sufficiently lacking in legitimacy and the political situation in industrial democracies is sufficiently fissile that, should there be further recessions, Eurozone calamities or stock market crashes, there is no surety that there may not be another 'government of the Left'.

Governing from the Left

Ironically, it was Harold Wilson who expressed most concisely what left-wing critics such as Ralph Miliband have long said about the British state: 'Whoever is in office, the Whigs are in power.'

The point doesn't have to be limited by its parochial frame of reference, however. Radical parties across the Continent, most recently Syriza, have discovered to their cost that to take office is not necessarily to take power. It is not just that there is something about states, senior civil servants, military leaders, Treasury advisors, Bank of England governors and so on, that makes them resistant to radical change. It is not just that to govern effectively requires a minimum of cooperation on the part of businesses and investors, as well as international trade institutions, ratings agencies, treaty organisations, and other powerful economic actors, which use what clout they have to veto reforms implemented by national governments. It is that there is an almost seamless circulation of power between them all. A radical government finds it difficult to wield power precisely because, if left to itself, it is rapidly encircled by those who actually hold power and who are accustomed to exercising it. Should it find a way to win time and space for its own agenda, the next obstacle it faces is that it somehow has to administer capitalism, while making it work for reform. That is, it has to find a growth formula that both makes capitalism grow, and profitably, while also transferring wealth and power to workers and the poor. In the twentieth century, the solution to this dilemma was a 'mixed economy', with public ownership, price and incomes policies, and a mildly redistributive welfare state. But that solution, insofar as it ever worked for radical ends, no longer works at all.

In the event that Corbyn were able to win an election, how is it possible in the twenty-first century to govern from the Left? It is not encouraging that the only major examples of relatively successful left-wing government in the twenty-first century all come from the 'pink tide' countries in Latin America, as the circumstances enabling those experiments to broadly work will not be repeated in Britain. The oil boom of the last decade, concurrent with years of high economic growth, was a crucial factor in funding the social programmes of the 'pink tide' governments. It gave them a vital space in which to experiment with ways of redistributing power, progressively reforming the state and engaging in economic intervention. A Corbyn-led government would be in the far less enviable situation of having to create significant economic growth without the benefit of a boom in assets to which it had access, in order to be able to make the considerable investments needed to confront social problems such as the housing crisis and rising poverty levels. At a time when businesses are still hoarding hundreds of billions of pounds rather than investing, the government would have to find a way to induce them to invest, since it cannot draw on the political clout that would be needed to simply tax the wealthy and nationalise the underperforming industries.

Labour under Corbyn does not as yet have the sort of coherent governing programme that it would need to achieve these objectives. Most Corbyn supporters are happy to accept, at this stage, that 'it's early days' – which is true enough. However, that is merely to underline the scale of the task given the consensus they are up against, and given the ways in which most Treasury officials, economics journalists, think tanks and financial institutions are inclined to construe the government's role in the economy. There are elements within the establishment in favour of some forms of mild economic intervention and stimulus spending along the lines that Corbyn and McDonnell favour. Lord Turner's 2013 speech to the Financial Services Authority, in which he called for what the Corbyn team would label a 'People's Quantitative Easing', was a clear signal that even some elements of the business establishment are growing tired of the austerity orthodoxy. However, the fact that there is a growing fringe of relatively far-sighted technocrats who are alarmed by Osborne's perpetuation of a model that is plainly not working does not mean that they would like to see a left-wing government implement these measures. In fact, it would be far easier for a right-wing government to achieve this in practice, than a government of the Left, whose measures would be treated as class war and provoke investor resistance.

It is also a matter of simple sociological realism that left-wing governments are just as subject to the pressures attendant on the effort to wield governmental power as any other party. Corbyn is already, necessarily, in a position of having to compromise – on Trident, Europe, nationalisation and other issues. The pressures that can be brought to bear from business leaders, civil servants, the media, international institutions, and his own parliamentary colleagues, should he actually have the chance to govern, will be considerable. Even if their persuasive powers are ultimately ineffective, Corbyn and McDonnell still face the problem that they cannot *force* businesses to invest. They are still in the same bind as previous social-democratic governments, which is that they aim to represent workers and the poor while necessarily, desperately needing the cooperation of business. Should Corbyn inherit an economy in recession and a government whose finances are in dire straits, he would face the choice of having to govern from a position of weakness, constant crisis, under fire from all sides, or of having to adjust and accept the orthodoxy, implement spending cuts and do as much as he can to humanise the worst effects of what he is compelled to do. The term for this, following on from 'Pasokification', is 'syrizafication', a process wherein the radical Left is swiftly chewed up and metabolised by the institutions it seeks to govern, becoming in effect an instrument of the neoliberal centre that it was elected to displace. The only possible counterpoint to such a scenario, and the inevitable unedifying cries of 'betrayal' that it would precipitate, would be a vibrant and mobilised grass-roots Left in the unions and beyond – a possible, yet by no means inevitable, political outcome.

Hopes of the Left

So what can Corbyn's supporters hope for? Labour Party members seem genuinely torn when pressed to answer such imponderables, pulled between the improbable fact of Corbyn's victory and the possibilities it seems to open up, and the imposing facts of the obstacles he must overcome. Some see a chance to move 'beyond nihilism and a Tory loafer stamping on a human face forever'. Others expect little but 'constant running battles, paralysis and turmoil'.[41]

But these questions can only be answered in relation to the big picture. And the big picture is one in which the decay of British democracy ironically creates new possibilities that could never have emerged when the two-party system was at its zenith. But it is also one wherein the decades of decline and degeneration in the size and activity of the union movement, the membership of the organised Left and the ideological profile of left-wing ideas will not be reversed in one miraculous breakthrough. There is, to be blunt, a generation of work to be done to reconstitute a viable, hab-itable Left and a powerful labour movement capable of at least curbing the power of business. But the timespan of the necessary interim will depend upon how effectively the Left is able to make use of the opportunities that are offered it, for these are the experiences through which a recomposition will or will not take place. To characterise the situation in this manner is to intentionally re-situate the conceptual focus from the customary short-termism of political analysis – in which the horizon of analysis is always this movement, this party conference, this election. The meaning and final success or failure of Corbynism will disclose itself in relation to this longer-term objective, as much as in relation to electoral outcomes, headlines and polls.

With this in mind, it seems likely that Corbyn's leadership will provide a temporary and much-needed space for the radical Left, wherein it can begin the work of regrouping and re-deploying its scattered forces. It probably will begin to shift the balance of opinion on a series of key matters, and it already deserves credit for the incomparable courage of its stance on immigration and refugees' rights. But unless the wider social and economic terrain changes dramatically in the years before 2020, it is unlikely to recoup enough of Labour's electoral losses to carry a general election. Even if it does, there is little in the way of a wider international climate – dominated, of course, by Washington and Wall Street – or the surrounding institutional framework, let alone in the business status quo, that would support and sustain an experimental radical-left form of government.

In all likelihood, Corbynism is a temporary phenomenon as far as Labour goes, and its most likely successor is some variation of the old Labour Right which will incorporate some of the milder elements of Corbynism – nationalising the rail, for example, or raising public investment – for its own purposes. If things go extremely well, Corbyn will have demonstrated to the right-wing of the party membership that they at least don't have to run in terror from a left-wing leadership, and will have enlarged the space in which the party's left-wing can openly, and to a limited degree influentially, organise. However, it seems likely that for the great majority of the newest recruits, Labour is a temporary home. Corbyn, flanked by a few allies but otherwise surrounded by a surprisingly resilient and bellicose old guard, can't keep the right-wing attack dogs on the back foot for too long. The political space for left-wing activists to operate effectively is likely to be closed before too long. There will be backlashes and disappointments, electoral setbacks and, in the event of government, continual, energy-sapping crises. In the final analysis, Corbynism will struggle to outrun the limits of Labourism. And it is those limits, above all, which have brought us to this impasse.

Notes

Introduction: Against All Odds

1   David Smith, 'Tony Blair admits he is baffled by rise of Bernie Sanders and Jeremy Corbyn', *Guardian*, 23 February 2016.

2   'Tony Blair: If your heart's with Jeremy Corbyn, get a transplant', *Guardian*, 22 July 2015; Peter Mandelson, 'The Labour Party is in mortal danger', *Financial Times*, 27 August 2015; Rowena Mason and Josh Halliday, 'Gordon Brown urges Labour not to be party of protest by choosing Jeremy Corbyn', *Guardian*, 17 August 2015.

3   Robert Mendick, 'Tony Blair gives Kazakhstan's autocratic president tips on how to defend a massacre', *Telegraph*, 24 August 2014.

4   Tony Benn, *Office Without Power: Diaries 1968–72*, London: Arrow, 1989.

5   Tony Benn, speech to the Engineering Union, AUEW Conference, May 1971. In Ruth Winstone, ed., *The Best of Benn: Letters, Diaries, Speeches and Other Writings*, London: Hutchinson, 2014, Kindle Loc. 621.

6   Hillary Wainwright and Leo Panitch, '"What we've achieved so far": an interview with Jeremy Corbyn', *Red Pepper*, December 2015.

7   Quoted in Nigel Cawthorne, *Jeremy Corbyn: Leading from the Left*, London: Endeavour Press Ltd, 2015, Kindle Loc. 180.

8   Rosa Prince, *Comrade Corbyn: A Very Unlikely Coup: How Jeremy Corbyn Stormed to the Labour Leadership*, London: Biteback Publishing, 2016.

9   Jessica Elgot, 'Jeremy Corbyn caught looking gloomy on night bus', *Guardian*, 1 August 2015.

10   Quoted in Nigel Cawthorne, *Jeremy Corbyn: Leading from the Left*, London: Endeavour Press Ltd, 2015, Kindle Loc. 238.

11   Jeremy Corbyn, 'Building the Social Movement', in Tom Unterrainer, ed., *Corbyn's Campaign*, Nottingham: Spokesman Books, 2016.

12   Hillary Wainwright and Leo Panitch, '"What we've achieved so far": an interview with Jeremy Corbyn', *Red Pepper*, December 2015.

13   Phil Burton-Cartledge, interview with the author, 19 February 2016.

14   Hardeep Matharu, 'Britain could be more left-wing than people assume, study finds', *The Independent*, 15 January 2016.

15   Sam Webb, 'Jeremy Corbyn gets hero's welcome at refugee rally on day he becomes Labour leader', *Mirror*, 12 September 2015.

16   Larry Elliott, 'OECD calls for less austerity and more public investment', *Guardian*, 18 February 2016.

17   Will Dahlgreen, 'British people keener on socialism than capitalism', *YouGov*, 23 February 2016.

1. How 'Project Fear' Failed

1   Michael Crick, @michaelcrick, Twitter, 28 May 2015, twitter.com/michaellcrick/status/603845352727453696.

2   'Labour leadership latest odds: can Jeremy Corbyn really win?', *Week*, 19 August 2015.

3   Cruddas's spin on the findings was reported by the *Guardian*'s resident Blairite, Patrick Wintour, with the following headline: 'Anti-austerity unpopular with voters, finds inquiry into Labour's election loss'. *Guardian*, 4 August 2015. In fact, the research did not 'find' any such thing.

4   Ross Hawkins, 'Ed Miliband did not lose election because he was too left wing – study', *BBC News*, 17 September 2015.

5   Steve Coogan, 'Andy Burnham is Labour's best hope', *Guardian*, 14 August 2015.

6   Interview with Marsha-Jane Thompson, 14 January 2016.

7   Interview with Ben Sellers, 12 February 2016.

8   Interview with Marsha-Jane Thompson, 14 January 2016.

9   Chi Onwurah, 'My nomination for leader of the Labour Party', Chionwurahmp.com, 11 June 2015.

10   Luke Akehurst, 'Why Jeremy Corbyn should be on the leadership ballot', *LabourList*, 9 June 2015.

11   The speech can be viewed at: 'Jeremy Corbyn – End Austerity Now – June 20 2015', YouTube, 20 June 2015.

12   Stephen Bush, 'Why are we so certain that Jeremy Corbyn can't win?', *New Statesman*, 23 June 2015.

13   Helen Pidd, 'Jeremy Corbyn: "Welcome to the mass movement of giving a toss about stuff "', *Guardian*, 30 August 2015.

14   Jon Stone, 'More people have joined Labour since the election than are in the entire Conservative party', *Independent*, 8 October 2015.

15   Interview with Marsha-Jane Thompson, 14 January 2016.

16   Interview with Ben Sellers, 12 February 2016.

17   Statistic quoted in Ben Sellers, '#JEZWEDID: From Red Labour to Jeremy Corbyn: A Tale from Social Media', in Tom Unterrainer, ed., *Corbyn's Campaign*, Nottingham: Spokesman Books, 2016.

18   Interview with Jeremy Gilbert, 19 January 2016.

19   Interview with Ben Sellers, 12 February 2016.

20   Kiran Moodley, 'The video which shows why Jeremy Corbyn is winning in the Labour leadership race', *Independent*, 23 July 2015.

21   Magpie Corvid, 'The Multitude of Fishes', *Salvage*, 3 September 2015, salvage.zone.

22   Interview with Marsha-Jane Thompson, 14 January 2016.

23   Nicholas Watt, 'Communication Workers Union backs Corbyn as antidote to Blairite "virus"', *Guardian*, 30 July 2015.

24   Tom Gordon, 'One year on: will Better Together change their tactics?', *Sunday Herald*, 23 June 2013.

25   Kiran Stacey, George Parker, Mure Dickie and Beth Rigby, 'Scottish referendum: How complacency nearly lost a united kingdom', *Financial Times*, 19 September 2014.

26   Nicholas Watt, Patrick Wintour and Severin Carrell, 'Scottish independence: Queen was asked to intervene amid yes vote fears', *Guardian*, 16 December 2015; Severin Carrell, 'Civil servants accused of bias during Scotland's independence referendum', *Guardian*, 23 March 2015; John Robertson, 'BBC bias and the Scots referendum – new report', *Open Democracy*, 21 February 2014.

27   Mikey Smith, 'Labour leadership race "should be halted" over hard-left "infiltrators"', *Mirror*, 26 July 2015; Glen Owen, 'Now top Labour

MP warns his party is on the brink of catastrophe', *Mail on Sunday*, 8 August 2015.

28 James Lyons and Robin Henry, 'Hard left plot to infiltrate Labour race', *Sunday Times*, 25 July 2015.

29 Dan Hodges, 'Jeremy Corbyn proves the lunatic wing of the Labour Party is still calling the shots', *Telegraph*, 15 June 2015; Dan Hodges, 'Sadiq Khan winning in London will be bad news for the Labour Party', *Telegraph*, 19 January 2016.

30 Andy McSmith, 'Jeremy Corbyn is a stranger to responsibility and will loathe leadership', *Independent*, 25 August 2015.

31 Andrew Sparrow, 'Miliband wins vote on Labour party reforms with overwhelming majority', *Guardian*, 1 March 2014.

32 Andrew Rawnsley, 'Ed Miliband boldly goes where even Tony Blair feared to tread', *Observer*, 2 February 2014.

33 Isabel Hardman, 'Labour "members" object to "purge"', *Spectator*, 20 August 2015; James Walsh and Frances Perraudin, 'Labour leadership election: rejected supporters express their anger', *Guardian*, 20 August 2015; Stephen Bush, 'Is Labour purging supporters of Jeremy Corbyn?', *New Statesman*, 20 August 2015; Oliver Wright and Matt Dathan, '#LabourPurge: Long-time supporters of party claim they have been barred from voting', *Independent*, 20 August 2015; Rowena Mason, 'Labour bans trade union head from voting in leadership election', *Guardian*, 25 August 2015; Peter Taheri and Kapil Komireddi, 'With up to 100,000 now barred, Labour has become less a broad church and more a secret society', *Independent*, 25 August 2015.

34 Louise Ridley, 'Jeremy Corbyn "Systematically" Attacked by British Press the Moment He Became Leader, Research Claims', *Huffington Post*, 26 November 2015.

35 Peter Dominiczak, Christopher Hope, Ben Riley-Smith and Kate McCann, 'Union bosses threaten to use Jeremy Corbyn's victory to cripple UK', *Telegraph*, 14 September 2015; Janet Daley, 'The hard Left wants to seize power on the streets, not at Westminster', *Telegraph*, 16 August 2015.

36 David Thomas, 'Prime Minister Corbyn… and the 1,000 days that destroyed Britain', *Daily Mail*, 22 August 2015.

37 Philip Stephens, 'Jeremy Corbyn for UK Labour party leader? Blame the bankers', *Financial Times*, 10 September 2015.

38   Editorial, 'The key questions Jeremy Corbyn must answer', *Jewish Chronicle*, 12 August 2015.

39   Eddy Portnoy, 'Simple, Offensive and Out There', *Forward*, 18 December 2008.

40   'Raed Salah Mahajna -v- The Secretary of State for the Home Department', Courts and Tribunals Judiciary, 10 April 2012, judiciary. gov.uk.

41   Dan Hodges, 'Jeremy Corbyn will be cheered by racists and terrorists', *Telegraph*, 25 August 2015; Simon Walters, 'Labour's "Mayor" savages Corbyn: Party star Khan damns leader over anti-Semitism', *Daily Mail*, 20 September 2015

42   Jonathan Freedland, 'The Corbyn tribe cares about identity, not power', *Guardian*, 24 July 2015; Suzanne Moore, 'Corbyn's Labour is a party without a point, led by a rebel with a cause', *Guardian*, 16 September 2015; Anne Perkins, 'Labour party members, please think before you vote for Jeremy Corbyn', *Guardian*, 22 July 2015; Anne Perkins, 'What the trials of Chris Froome can teach us about Jeremy Corbyn', *Guardian*, 23 July 2015.

43   Andrew Rawnsley, 'Why Labour is gravitating towards the Conservatives' dream candidate', *Observer*, 19 July 2015; Andrew Rawnsley, 'Labour downs a deadly cocktail of fatalism, fury and fantasy', *Observer*, 26 July 2015.

44   Ed Vulliamy, 'Why I take issue with the Observer's stance on Jeremy Corbyn', *Observer*, 20 September 2015.

45   Andrew Sparrow, 'Labour donor: Jeremy Corbyn win could cause SDP-style split', *Guardian*, 24 July 2015.

46   Polly Toynbee, 'In Labour's leadership race, Yvette Cooper is the one to beat', *Guardian*, 23 June 2015.

47   Editorial, 'The Guardian view on Labour's choice: Corbyn has shaped the campaign, but Cooper can shape the future', *Guardian*, 13 August 2015; Selma James and Nina Lopez, 'Yvette Cooper supported sexist austerity; Jeremy Corbyn has always opposed it', Letters page, *Guardian*, 18 August 2015.

48   Suzanne Moore, 'As Jeremy Corbyn was anointed leader, not one female voice was heard', *Guardian*, 12 September 2015.

49   Will Dahlgreen, 'With one month to go, Corbyn's lead increases', *YouGov*, 10 August 2015.

50   Daisy Benson, 'If it's truly progressive, Labour will have voted in a female leader – regardless of her policies', *Independent*, 11 September 2015.

51   Michael Wilkinson, 'Has Jeremy Corbyn got a woman problem?', *Telegraph*, 14 December 2015.

52   Cathy Newman, 'Welcome to Jeremy Corbyn's blokey Britain – where "brocialism" rules', *Telegraph*, 14 September.

53   This is reported, albeit grudgingly, in the *Independent*. Matt Dathan, 'Jeremy Corbyn comes out fighting amid sexism row and insists shadow Cabinet positions he has given to women are the real "top jobs"', *Independent*, 14 September 2015.

54   John Elledge, 'Labour chooses white man as leader', *New Statesman*, 12 September 2015.

55   Andrew Grice and Oliver Wright, 'A third of Labour voters less likely to vote for the party with Jeremy Corbyn in charge, with critics already plotting to oust him', *Independent*, 18 September 2015.

56   Allister Heath, 'One Thing Is Clear – Jeremy Corbyn Has No Understanding of the British People', *Telegraph*, 30 September 2015.

57   Rafael Behr, 'In Oldham, Jeremy Corbyn is just another face of "poncified" Labour', *Guardian*, 2 December 2015.

58   Roy Greenslade, 'The Times counts the cost of spinning against Labour in Oldham', *Guardian*, 4 December 2015.

59   John Harris, John Domokos and Dan Susman, 'Oldham byelection: Corbynmania collides with reality – video', *Guardian*, 2 December.

60   Asa Bennett, 'Oldham by-election: did Muslims worried about war in Syria save Jeremy Corbyn from doom?', *Telegraph*, 4 December 2015.

61   Kate McCann and Rosa Silverman, 'Revealed: Jeremy Corbyn had a second relationship with a Labour politician', *Telegraph*, 18 September 2015.

62   Janet Daley, 'I've lived under Jeremy Corbyn's rule – it turned me into a Tory', *Telegraph*, 25 July 2015.

63   Anne Perkins, 'The National Anthem May Stick in Corbyn's Craw, but It Is His Job to Sing It', *Guardian*, 16 September 2015.

64   Aubrey Allegretti, 'The Sun's Front Page Smear Story On "Hypocrite" Jeremy Corbyn Revealed As False', *Huffington Post*, 15 September 2015.

65   Liam Young, 'Why is the Sun so determined to destroy Jeremy Corbyn? Because he could be prime minister', *New Statesman*, 9 December 2015.

66   Roy Greenslade, 'Rightwing press mounts assault over Jeremy Corbyn's Cenotaph nod', *Guardian*, 9 November 2015.

67   Rowena Mason, 'Corbyn urged to disband Momentum after Labour MPs report bullying and abuse', *Guardian*, 3 December 2015; Charlie Cooper, 'Syria air strikes: Pro-war MPs bullied by extremists, say Labour figures', *Independent*, 2 December 2015; Cathy Newman, 'Showing Corbyn how it's done: The war Britain's bullied female MPs are determined to win', *Telegraph*, 3 December 2015; Roy Greenslade, 'Stella Creasy crushes story about protest outside her house', *Guardian*, 4 December 2015.

68   Rowena Mason, 'Corbyn urged to disband Momentum after Labour MPs report bullying and abuse', *Guardian*, 3 December 2015.

69   Tom Tugenhat MP, 'Jeremy Corbyn is no pacifist – he wants to see Britain defeated', *Telegraph*, 18 January 2016.

70   Caroline Mortimer, 'British Army "could stage mutiny under Corbyn", says senior serving general', *Independent*, 20 September 2015.

71   Rowena Mason and Patrick Wintour, 'Trident: military chief will not be disciplined over Corbyn remarks', *Guardian*, 9 November 2015; Andrew Sparrow, 'Corbyn to complain to MoD about army chief's "political interference"', *Guardian*, 9 November 2015.

72   Philip Collins, 'Am I angry at vain, arrogant Ed? Hell, yes', *Times*, 15 May 2015.

73   Tim Stanley, 'Labour didn't lose because it was too Left-wing. But it will lose again if it becomes too Right-wing', *Telegraph*, 15 May 2015.

74   Tony Blair, 'In conversation with … Tony Blair: opening remarks', *Progress*, 22 July 2015.

75   Dan Hodges, 'Sadiq Khan Winning in London Will Be Bad News for the Labour Party', *Telegraph*, 19 January 2016.

76   Peter Hyman, 'This Is an Existential Moment in Labour's History. It May Not Survive. And It May Never Win Again', *Guardian*, 20 December 2015.

77   Polly Toynbee, 'Dear Labour, split the party and you'll regret it. Love from an sdp candidate', *Guardian*, 26 January 2016.

78   Jon Rentoul, 'Daily catch-up: Will the Labour Party split? Will there be an SDP Mark II?', *Independent*, 14 December 2015.

79   Mark Mardell, 'Is "King Jeremy the Accidental" on the up?', *BBC News*, 21 January 2016.

80   Robin De Peyer, 'Noel Gallagher launches scathing attack on Jeremy Corbyn's Labour leadership', *Evening Standard*, 10 January 2016.

81   Peter Hyman, 'This is an existential moment in Labour's history. It may not survive. And it may never win again', *Guardian*, 20 December 2015.

82   Interview with Jeremy Gilbert, 14 January 2016.

83   Peter Mandelson, 'Peter Mandelson's memo on how Labour's modernisers lost their way – and where they go next', *New Statesman*, 25 September 2010.

84   This is not to deny that New Labour generated a degree of positive support among some voters – especially among ex-Conservative voters on economic issues. However, Labour's biggest asset was the 'new equilibrium' reached by Tories in the polls after the ERM crisis. Peter Kellner, 'Why the Tories Were Trounced', *Parliamentary Affairs*, vol. 50, no. 4, 1997.

85   Rowena Mason, 'Jeremy Corbyn is most popular among voters from all parties, poll suggests', *Guardian*, 15 August 2015; Joe Murphy, 'Left-winger Jeremy Corbyn is "first choice for Londoners"', *Evening Standard*, 14 August 2015.

86   Roy Hattersley, 'Labour's moderates have a duty to serve in the shadow cabinet', *Guardian*, 13 September 2015.

87   John McDonnell, 'How Labour will secure the high-wage, hi-tech economy of the future', *Guardian*, 19 November 2015.

88   Even Paul Kenny of the GMB, who is otherwise sceptical of Corbyn, insists that the Blairites should accept Corbyn's victory or quit the party. Jon Craig, 'Union Leaders Say "Accept Corbyn Or Quit"', *Sky News*, 12 September 2015.

89   When New Labour first promoted the replacement of Trident, an overwhelming majority of the public opposed renewing it. See 'Nuclear Deterrent', *Populus*, 21–22 February 2007. In subsequent polls, a majority of the public favoured getting rid of Trident to save money. See: 'Published Voting Intention Figures', *ComRes*, 4–6 September 2009; Glen Owen, 'Here's £37bn of cuts to get you started, voters tell PM', *Mail on Sunday*, 13 June 2010. More recent polling suggests that opinion is at least an even split on Trident. Andrew Grice, 'Trident: Majority of Britons back keeping nuclear weapons programme, poll shows', *Independent*, 24 January 2016. Meanwhile, a number of leading ex-generals have publicly called for the scrapping of Trident. 'Generals in

"scrap Trident" call', *BBC News*, 16 January 2009; Helen Pidd, 'Trident nuclear missiles are £20bn waste of money, say generals', *Guardian*, 16 January 2009; Kate Hudson, 'Trident's an outdated waste. Even the military say so', *New Statesman*, 24 June 2015.

2. The Crisis of British Politics

1 Oliver Milne, 'Momentum sweeps board at Labour party youth elections', *Guardian*, 19 February 2016

2 I am grateful to Simon Hewitt for these points. Interview with the author, 13 January 2016.

3 Quoted in Ian Dunt, 'Ed Miliband: We need our working class vote back', *Politics.co.uk*, 16 August 2010. Although, in fact, this argument was slightly over-simplified. Millions of those who had voted Labour in 1997 would have died by 2010. The question is why those voters weren't replaced. The biggest reason is that voters who might tend to support Labour – largely poor and largely young – stopped turning out. For a more conventionally Blairite take on the numbers, see Peter Kellner, 'Labour's lost votes', *Prospect*, 17 October 2012.

4 Jon Trickett reaffirmed this argument after the 2015 election defeat. 'It was the working class, not the middle class that sunk Labour', *New Statesman*, 13 May 2015.

5 Toby Helm, 'Labour's lost voters may never return again, study finds', *Guardian*, 18 July 2015.

6 Ross Hawkins, 'Ed Miliband did not lose election because he was too left wing – study', *BBC News*, 17 September 2015; Rowena Mason, 'Beckett report: Labour lost election over economy, immigration and benefits', *Guardian*, 14 January 2016.

7 Alberto Nardelli, 'Party membership in the UK is tiny', *Guardian*, 29 September 2014; Hugh Pemberton and Mark Wickham-Jones, 'Labour's lost grassroots: the rise and fall of party membership', *British Politics*, vol. 8, 2013.

8 John Moylan, 'Union membership has halved since 1980', *BBC News*, 7 September 2012; Brian Groom, 'UK trade union membership holds steady', *Financial Times*, 20 May 2014; Michael J Morely, Patrick Gunnigle, David G Collings, *Global Industrial Relations*, Routledge, Abingdon, 2006, p. 226; also Robert J Flanagan, *Globalization and Labor*

Conditions: Working Conditions and Worker Rights in a Global Economy, Oxford University Press, Oxford, 2006.

9   Richard Hyman, 'Strikes in the UK: withering away?', *EurWork: European Observatory of Working Life*, 27 July 1999.

10 James Doran, '5 Things You Need to Know About "Pasokification"', *Novara Media*, 5 January 2015.

11 The loss of ethnic minority voters was apparent well before Corbyn took the leadership. See Tim Wigmore, 'Is Labour losing the ethnic minority vote?', *New Statesman*, 5 January 2015. The evidence of polling, however, suggests that Corbyn's leadership is less popular among these groups than Labour is as a whole. Aaron Bastani, 'Corbyn's declining popularity?', *LRB blog*, 3 December 2015.

12 Colin Crouch, *Coping with Post-Democracy*, Fabian Society, 2000; Colin Crouch, *Post-Democracy*, London: Polity, 2004; Colin Crouch, *The Strange Non-Death of Neo-Liberalism*, London: Polity, 2011.

13 Peter Mair, *Ruling the Void: The Hollowing Out of Western Democracy*, London: Verso, 2013, Kindle Loc. 367.

14 Peter Mair, *Ruling the Void: The Hollowing Out of Western Democracy*, London: Verso, 2013, Kindle Loc. 437–67.

15 Armin Schäfer and Wolfgang Streeck, 'Introduction: Politics in the Age of Austerity', in Armin Schäfer and Wolfgang Streeck, eds., *Politics in the Age of Austerity*, Cambridge: Polity, p. 16.

16 Peter Mair, *Ruling the Void: The Hollowing Out of Western Democracy*, London: Verso, 2013, Kindle Loc. 665.

17 Peter Mair, *Ruling the Void: The Hollowing Out of Western Democracy*, London: Verso, 2013, Kindle Loc. 623.

18 Pippa Norris, 'Apathetic Landslide', *Parliamentary Affairs*, 54, 2001, pp. 565–89.

19 Pippa Norris, 'Apathetic Landslide', *Parliamentary Affairs*, 54, 2001, pp. 565–89; Ron Johnson and Charles Pattie, *Putting Voters in Their Place: geography and elections in Great Britain*, Oxford: Oxford University Press, 2006, p. 246.

20 David Garner, 'Why do so few people vote in UK elections now?', Department of Politics, University of York, 20 June 2005.

21 Emma Ailes, 'Election 2015: Who are the non-voters?', *BBC News*, 6 May 2015.

22 Roger Mortimore and Kully Kaur-Ballagan, 'Ethnic Minority Voters and

Non-Voters at the 2005 British General Election', Ipsos-Mori, Paper for EPOP Conference, University of Nottingham, September 2006; 'General Election 2015 explained: Turnout', *Independent*, 4 May 2015.

23 On these origins, see Daron Acemoglu and James A Robinson, 'Why Did the West Extend the Franchise? Democracy, Inequality and Growth in Historical Perspective', Cambridge, MA: MIT Press, 1998, web.mit. edu.

24 Wolfgang Streeck, *Buying Time: The Delayed Crisis of Democratic Capitalism*, London: Verso, 2014, pp. 77–9.

25 On the relationship between neoliberals, democracy and the far right, see: William E. Scheuerman, *Carl Schmitt: The End of Law*, Lanham MD: Rowman & Littlefield, 1999; Renato Christi, *Carl Schmitt and Authoritarian Liberalism: Strong State, Free Economy*, University of Wales Press, Cardiff, 1998; Perry Anderson, 'The Intransigent Right' in *Spectrum: from right to left in the world of ideas*, Verso, 2005, pp. 15–16; and Renée Sallas, 'Friedrich von Hayek, Leader and Master of Liberalism', *El Mercurio*, 12 April 1981. On the role of neoliberals in the Pinochet dictatorship, see David Harvey, *Neoliberalism: A Short History*, Oxford: Oxford University Press, 2005, pp. 7–9; Naomi Klein, *The Shock Doctrine: The Rise of Disaster Capitalism*, New York: Metropolitan Books, 2007, pp. 77–87; Greg Grandin, 'The Road from Serfdom: Milton Friedman and the Economics of Empire', *Counterpunch*, 17 November 2006. And on the underlying assumptions of neoliberal thought with regard to state and economy, see: Philip Mirowski, *Never Let a Serious Crisis Go to Waste: How Neoliberalism Survived the Financial Meltdown*, London: Verso, 2013; Philip Mirowski, 'On the Origins (at Chicago) of some Species of Neoliberal Evolutionary Economics', in Robert van Horn, Philip Mirowski and Thomas A Stapleford, eds., *Building Chicago Economics: New Perspectives on the History of America's Most Powerful Economics Program*, Cambridge University Press, 2011.

26 James M. Buchanan, *Public Finance in Democratic Process: Fiscal Institutions and Individual Choice*, Chapel Hill, NC: UNC Press, 1967; William A. Niskanen, Jr., *Bureaucracy and Representative Government*, AldineTransaction, 2007; William A. Niskanen Jr., *Bureaucracy and Public Economics*, Edward Elgar Publishing Ltd., 1996.

27 Rarely a year goes by when some scandal does not befall Serco, by far one of the most useless corporations in the world, and also the

government's favourite. Richard Whitell and Emily Dugan, 'Services provider established by outsourcing giant Serco overcharged NHS by millions', *Independent*, 27 August 2014; 'Prisons privatisation cancelled amid Serco probe', *BBC News*, 22 November 2013. Competition in the NHS was found to have driven up overheads to 15 per cent of total costs by 2007. See Steffie Woolhandler and David U. Himmelstein, 'Competition in a publicly funded healthcare system', *British Medical Journal*, 335, 2007.

28 Colin Crouch, *Coping with Post-Democracy*, Fabian Society, 2000.

29 Mark Mills, 'British Businesses Are Hoarding Billions That Could Be Invested in SMEs', *Huffington Post*, 3 January 2014; Adam Davidson, 'Why are Corporations Hoarding Trillions?', *New York Times*, 20 January 2016.

30 An extended version of this argument can be found in Richard Seymour, *Against Austerity: How We Can Fix the Crisis They Made*, London: Pluto Press, 2014.

31 Peter Mair, *Ruling the Void: The Hollowing Out of Western Democracy*, London: Verso, 2013, Kindle Loc. 367 & 1327.

32 Frances Perraudin and Rowena Mason, 'Include Lib Dems in coalition or face second election this year, says Clegg', *Guardian*, 5 May 2015.

33 Emma Ailes, 'Election 2015: Who are the non-voters?', *BBC News*, 6 May 2015.

34 'Building Public Engagement: Options for Developing Select Committee Outreach, First Special Report of Session 2015–16 (House of Commons Papers)'. House of Commons Liaison Committee. November 2005

35 Polly Toynbee, 'Every vote counts – to waste yours would be near-criminal', *Guardian*, 7 May 2015; Iain Sinclair, 'Polly Toynbee, Jeremy Corbyn and the limits of acceptable politics', *Open Democracy*, 29 June 2015.

36 In the Iowa primary, which was unexpectedly a near draw, Sanders defeated Clinton 6–1 among under thirties. See Aaron Bastani, 'Young Americans', *LRB blog*, 10 February 2016.

37 Gerassimos Moschonas, *In the Name of Social Democracy: The Great Transformation 1945 to the Present*, London: Verso, 2002, pp. 190–204. On the struggle throughout the 1980s to defend a non-neoliberal set of institutional commitments, see Göran Therborn, *Why Some People*

Are More Unemployed Than Others: The Strange Paradox of Growth and Unemployment, London: Verso, 1986.

38 This analysis draws extensively from Paolo Chiocchetti's as-yet-unpublished PhD thesis, 'Filling the Vacuum?: The Development of the Partisan Radical Left in Germany, France and Italy, 1989–2013', Department of European and International Studies, King's College London, 14 November 2013. I am also grateful to the author for explaining his thesis in personal conversation. But see also: Dan Hough, Michael Koß and Jonathan Olsen, *The Left Party in Contemporary German Politics*, London: Palgrave Macmillan, 2007; Dan Hough, Michael Koß and Jonathan Olsen, *Left Parties in National Governments*, London: Palgrave Macmillan, 2010; Kate Hudson, *European Communism since 1989: Towards a New European Left?*, Palgrave Macmillan, 2000; Kate Hudson, *The New European Left: A Socialism for the Twenty-First Century?*, Palgrave Macmillan, 2012; Valeria Camia, 'Social democrats, Europe and the radical party factor', National Centre of Competence in Research (NCCR), *Challenges to Democracy in the Twenty-First Century*, Working Paper No. 54, July 2012; Daniele Albertazzi, Clodagh Brook and Charlotte Ross, 'Italy's radical Left in the Age of Berlusconi', *Radical Politics Today*, July 2009; Luke March and Cas Mudde, 'What's Left of the Radical Left? The European Radical Left After 1989: Decline and Mutation', *Comparative European Politics*, 3, 2005; Luke March, *Contemporary Far Left Parties in Europe*, Berlin: Friedrich-Ebert-Stiftung, 2008; Luke March, *Radical Left Parties in Europe*, London: Routledge, 2011.

3. Labour Isn't Working: Whatever Happened to Social Democracy?

1 Tony Blair, 'In defence of Blairism, by Tony Blair', *Spectator*, 9 December 2015.

2 On the role of religious ideas in the formation of Labour, see Mark Bevir, *The Making of British Socialism*, Princeton, NJ: Princeton University Press, 2011.

3 Though not the disappearance of the Chartist idea. See Keith Flett, *Chartism After 1848: The Working Class and the Politics of Radical Education*, Pontypool: Merlin Press, 2006.

4   Quoted in John Saville, *The Labour Movement in Britain: A Commentary*, London: Faber & Faber, 1988, p. 9.

5   Maurice Cowling, *1867: Disraeli, Gladstone and Revolution: The Passing of the Second Reform Bill*, Cambridge University Press, 2005, pp. 48–52; Paul Foot, *The Vote: How it Was Won and How it Was Undermined*, Viking, 2005, pp. 125–9; John Ramden, *An Appetite for Power: A History of the Conservative Party Since 1830*, HarperCollins, 1998, p. 93.

6   Gordon Phillips, *The Rise of the Labour Party: 1893–1931*, London: Routledge, 1992, p. 7.

7   Gordon Phillips, *The Rise of the Labour Party: 1893–1931*, London: Routledge, 1992, p. 9.

8   Gregory Elliott, *Labourism and the English Genius: The Strange Death of Labour England?*, London: Verso, 1993, p. 27.

9   Ross McKibbin, *Parties and People: England 1914–1951*, Oxford: Oxford University Press, 2010, pp. 3–5.

10   Paul Mason's description of the syndicalist milieu, from 1899 to 1914, is apt: 'All over the world, "labour of the humbler kind" was getting organised. If the Paris Commune had closed the door on the era of street revolutions, the dock strike had opened an era of workplace revolutions. The trade union itself could become a mini-commune: training and educating workers for self-government'. Paul Mason, *Live Working or Die Fighting: How the Working Class Went Global*, London: Vintage Books, 2007, p. 117.

11   Ralph Miliband, *Parliamentary Socialism: A Study in the Politics of Labour*, New York: Monthly Review Press, 1964, p. 43.

12   Tudor Jones, *Remaking the Labour Party: From Gaitskell to Blair*, London: Routledge, 1996, pp. 4–5.

13   Gregory Elliott, *Labourism and the English Genius: The Strange Death of Labour England?*, London: Verso, 1993, p. 33.

14   Ross McKibbin, *Parties and People: England 1914–1951*, Oxford: Oxford University Press, 2010, pp. 29–30.

15   Andrew Thorpe, *A History of the British Labour Party: Third Edition*, Basingstoke: Palgrave Macmillan, 2008, pp. 59–60.

16   Ralph Miliband, *Parliamentary Socialism: A Study in the Politics of Labour*, New York: Monthly Review Press, 1964, pp. 103–4.

17   Gregory Elliott, *Labourism and the English Genius: The Strange Death of Labour England?*, London: Verso, 1993, p. 38.

18   Ralph Miliband, *Parliamentary Socialism: A Study in the Politics of Labour*, New York: Monthly Review Press, 1964, p. 108

19   Ralph Miliband, *Parliamentary Socialism: A Study in the Politics of Labour*, New York: Monthly Review Press, 1964, p. 112

20   Ralph Miliband, *Parliamentary Socialism: A Study in the Politics of Labour*, New York: Monthly Review Press, 1964, pp. 128–36; Andrew Thorpe, *A History of the British Labour Party: Third Edition*, Basingstoke: Palgrave Macmillan, 2008, p. 66.

21   Matthew Worley, *Labour Inside the Gate: A History of the British Labour Party Between the Wars*, London: IB Tauris, 2009, p. 123.

22   Donald Sassoon, *One Hundred Years of Socialism: The West European Left in the Twentieth Century*, London: IB Tauris, p. 57; Matthew Worley, *Labour Inside the Gate: A History of the British Labour Party Between the Wars*, London: IB Tauris, 2009, pp. 123–5.

23   Gregory Elliott, *Labourism and the English Genius: The Strange Death of Labour England?*, London: Verso, 1993, pp. 43–5.

24   See Ross McKibbin, *Classes and Cultures: 1918–1951*, Oxford: Oxford University Press, 2000, pp. 38–40.

25   Adam Przeworski, *Capitalism and Social Democracy*, Cambridge: Cambridge University Press, 1985, p. 33.

26   Steven Fielding, 'What Did 'The People' Want?: The Meaning of the 1945 General Election', *The Historical Journal*, vol 35, no 3 (Sep., 1992), pp. 623–39; Ralph Miliband, *Parliamentary Socialism: A Study in the Politics of Labour*, New York: Monthly Review Press, 1964, pp. 272–4; Henry Pelling, 'The 1945 General Election Reconsidered', *The Historical Journal*, vol. 23, no. 2 (Jun., 1980), pp. 399–414.

27   On the wartime reconfiguration of the state, see Paul Addison, *The Road to 1945: British politics and the Second World War*, London: Pimlico, 1994.

28   Kevin Jefferies, *The Churchill Coalition and Wartime Politics, 1940–1945*, Manchester: Manchester University Press, 1995, pp. 60–3.

29   Ina Zweiniger-Bargielowska, 'Rationing, Austerity and the Conservative Party Recovery after 1945', *The Historical Journal*, vol. 37, no. 1, 1994; David Seawright, 'One Nation', in Kevin Hickson, ed., *The Political Thought of the Conservative Party Since 1945*, Basingstoke: Palgrave Macmillan, 2005.

30   On the revisionist current, see Tudor Jones, *Remaking the Labour Party: From Gaitskell to Blair*, London: Routledge, 1996.

31   Quoted in John Saville, *The Labour Movement in Britain: A Commentary*, London: Faber & Faber, 1988, p. 105.

32   Figure quoted in John Saville, 'The Labour Government (1967)', in David Coates, ed., *Paving the Third Way: The Critique of Parliamentary Socialism*, London: The Merlin Press Ltd, 2003.

33   On this, the most concise background is given by Paul Gilroy and Joe Simm, 'Law, order and the state of the left', *Capital and Class*, 9 (Spring, 1985), pp. 15–55.

34   Peter Weller, 'British Labour and the Cold War: The Foreign Policy of the Labour Governments, 1945–1951', *Journal of British Studies*, vol. 26, no. 1, England's Foreign Relations (Jan., 1987), pp. 54–82.

35   John Newsinger, *British Counterinsurgency: From Palestine to Northern Ireland*, Basingstoke: Palgrave Macmillan, 2002.

36   Stuart Hall, 'The Battle for Socialist Ideas in the 1980s', *Socialist Register*, 1982.

37   Two Keynesian economists offer an acerbic critique of the post-war record of Labour. See Larry Elliott and Dan Atkinson, *The Age of Insecurity*, London: Verso, 1999. On the greatly exaggerated role of 'planning' in post-war Britain, see Nigel Harris, *Competition and the Corporate Society: British Conservatives, the State and Industry 1945–1964*, Abingdon: Routledge, 2013.

38   Martin Pugh, *Speak for Britain!: A New History of the Labour Party*, London: Vintage Books, 2011, p. 359–60.

39   Andrew Thorpe, *A History of the British Labour Party: Third Edition*, Basingstoke: Palgrave Macmillan, 2008, pp. 169–170.

40   Gregory Elliott, *Labourism and the English Genius: The Strange Death of Labour England?*, London: Verso, 1993, pp. 75–6.

41   Richard Crossman, *The Diaries of a Cabinet Minister: Lord President of the Council and Leader of the House of Commons, 1966–68*, Hamilton, 1976, p. 587.

42   On the 'new racism' pioneered by Powell and others, see Martin Barker, *The New Racism*, London: Junction Books, 1981.

43   Stuart Hall, 'Thatcherism – Rolling Back the Welfare State', *Thesis Eleven*, vol. 7, no. 1 (February 1983), pp. 6–19.

44   This opposition between 'state' and 'market' has always been highly misleading. Markets are not, and never have been, self-generating or self-sustaining: they are politically and legally constituted. Their

spread and their global connectedness has been expedited by strong, interventionist states. See Leo Panitch and Sam Gindin, *The Making of Global Capitalism: The Political Economy of American Empire*, London: Verso, 2013. At any rate, it is not quite correct to speak of 'the market' as if this exhaustively described the capitalism which Labour governments have sought to reform. And if, following Marx, we depart the noisy sphere of circulation and trade, and enter the hidden abode of production, we tend to find the state's fingerprints everywhere. From tax breaks to subsidies to diplomacy and espionage, much of modern industry would be impossible without the continual coddling, nurturing and leadership of national states. The Apple corporation would, for example, be considerably less of a global giant were it not for the technologies made available to it by years of public sector investment and research, and the markets in labour and goods opened to it by aggressive US diplomacy. Mariana Mazzucato, *The Entrepreneurial State: Debunking Public vs. Private Myths in Risk and Innovation*, London, New York: Anthem Press, 2013. In short, the issue is never 'state intervention or not?', but always 'what kind of state intervention?'. This has been obscured both by Thatcherites, who claim an 'anti-statist' mantle, and Blairites, who try to distinguish their programme from Conservatism by reference to their acknowledgement of the role of government.

45   Patrick Bell, *The Labour Party in Opposition 1970–1974*, London: Routledge, 2004; Martin Pugh, *Speak for Britain!: A New History of the Labour Party*, London: Vintage Books, 2011, p. 370–1.

46   Tony Benn, Speech to the Engineering Union, AUEW Conference, May 1971. In Ruth Winstone, ed., *The Best of Benn: Letters, Diaries, Speeches and Other Writings*, London: Hutchinson, 2014, Kindle Loc. 621–733.

47   Wyn Grant, 'Business Interests and the British Conservative Party', *Government and Opposition*, vol 15, no. 2, 1980.

48   The idea of enforcing workers' representation in company boards was supported by the Bullock Report of 1977, one of the first major turning points in the conversion of business to Thatcherism, but the plans were never likely to be implemented. In fact, moreover, Benn also had difficulty in gaining the support of trade unionist for industrial democracy, on the grounds that they felt such methods of inclusion were intended

to obstruct or replace the exercise of real, rank-and-file power. See David Powell, *Tony Benn: A Political Life*, London: Continuum, 2003, pp. 122–3.

49   Stuart Hall, 'The Great Moving Right Show', in Stuart Hall and Martin Jacques, eds., *The Politics of Thatcherism*, London: Lawrence & Wishart, 1983.

50   Stuart Hall, Chas Critcher, Tony Jefferson, John Clarke and Brian Roberts, *Policing The Crisis: Mugging, The State, and Law and Order*, London: Macmillan, 1978.

51   Andrew Gamble provides an authoritative account of Thatcherite ideology and what might be called its 'rational kernel' in *The Free Economy and the Strong State: The Politics of Thatcherism*, London: Palgrave Macmillan, 1994.

52   Sir Ian Gilmour, quoted in Eric J Evans, *Thatcher and Thatcherism*, London: Routledge, 2004, p. 14.

53   Neil Rollings, 'Cracks in the Post-War Keynesian Settlement? The Role of Organised Business in Britain in the Rise of Neoliberalism Before Margaret Thatcher', *Twentieth Century British History*, vol. 24, no. 4, 2013, pp. 637–59.

54   Martin Pugh, *Speak for Britain!: A New History of the Labour Party*, London: Vintage Books, 2011, p. 365.

55   Martin Pugh, *Speak for Britain!: A New History of the Labour Party*, London: Vintage Books, 2011, p. 371.

56   A general tendency, if culpably exaggerated by the centrist intellectuals and politicians, in European social democracy. See Gerassimos Moschonas, *In the Name of Social Democracy: The Great Transformation, 1954 to the Present*, London: Verso, 2002.

57   First-past-the-post converted 42 per cent of the vote in 1983 and 1987, into 62 per cent and 58 per cent of the parliamentary seats, respectively.

58   As Tim Bale put it, Thatcher won not because she persuaded a majority of people of her views, but because the macroeconomic conditions were sufficiently congenial for a sufficient plurality of people at just the right times. Tim Bale, *The Conservative Party: From Thatcher to Cameron*, London: Polity, p. 24. On shifting social attitudes under Thatcher and their electoral manifestations, see Anthony Heath, Roger Jowell, and John Curtice, 'Understanding Electoral Change in Britain', *Parliamentary Affairs*, Oxford University Press, 1986.

59   Stuart Hall, 'The 'Little Caesars' of Social Democracy', *Marxism Today*, April 1981.

4. New Labour and Corbyn's Route to Power

1   Quoted in Samuel Beer, 'Liberalism Rediscovered', *The Economist*, 7 February 1998.

2   Quoted in Martin Pugh, *Speak for Britain!: A New History of the Labour Party*, London: Vintage Books, 2011, p. 419.

3   Jon Stone, 'Liz Kendall says she lost the Labour leadership election because she was the "eat your greens" candidate', *Independent*, 26 January 2016.

4   John Reid is quoted lauding 'Labour hegemony' at the moment of the Iraq invasion in Andrew Pearmain, *The Politics of New Labour: A Gramscian Analysis*, London: Lawrence & Wishart, 2011, Kindle Loc. 235; Peter Hyman describes the rough contours of this 'hegemony' in 'This is an existential moment in Labour's history. It may not survive. And it may never win again', *Guardian*, 20 December 2015. As Pearmain points out, these ways of construing Gramsci's concept of hegemony are bowdlerised and narrowly focused on electoral party politics in a way that has little to do with any rigorous use of the idea.

5   By far the most historically and theoretically detailed account of these origins is Andrew Pearmain, *The Politics of New Labour: A Gramscian Analysis*, London: Lawrence & Wishart, 2011.

6   A fairly typical settling of accounts with the Left over its failure to recognise these changes can be found in Stuart Hall, 'The Culture Gap', *Marxism Today*, January 1984; and Stuart Hall, 'The Meaning of New Times', in David Morley and Kuan-Hsing Chen, eds., *Stuart Hall: Critical Dialogues in Cultural Studies*, Abingdon: Routledge, 1996. Hall would later recant on some of this line of argument, arguing that 'there was that odd moment, when the critique went overboard, when we almost hero-ized consumption and designer capitalism'. Quoted in Pearmain, *The Politics of New Labour: A Gramscian Analysis*, London: Lawrence & Wishart, 2011, Kindle Loc. 1597.

7   The case for realignment, to exclude the hard-Left, was put by Hall in characteristically mollifying tones. It was not about trying to expel enemies or create a monolithic culture, but about repudiating

'the "hard-Left" as a peculiar and distinctive political style, a set of habits, a political-cultural tradition, stretching right across the actual organisational sub-divisions of the Left'. The results were, of course, quite other. Stuart Hall, 'Realignment – for What?', *Marxism Today*, December 1985.

8   Pearmain notes that Marxism Today in the eighties was 'mesmerised and on occasions plainly excited by what Martin Jacques still calls its "power and strength"'. *The Politics of New Labour: A Gramscian Analysis*, London: Lawrence & Wishart, 2011, Kindle Loc. 1597–628. Once Blair took the helm of Labour, a sign of its forced adaptation to Thatcherism's 'power and strength', Hall saluted the 'necessary' changes that New Labour signalled for the Labour Party. Stuart Hall, 'Parties on the verge of a nervous breakdown', *Soundings*, no 1, Autumn 1995. As late as 1996, Hall et al. were inclined to cautiously welcome New Labour's policy developments. Editorial, 'What is at stake?', *Soundings*, no. 2, Spring 1996; by the following year, the disillusionment had thoroughly set in, and was explored in a series of brutally pessimistic analyses, beginning with a pre-election piece written by Hall and Jacques on New Labour for *Guardian*, 'Tony Blair: The Greatest Tory since Margaret Thatcher?'. Later pieces theorised the changing analysis in a distinctively Gramscian idiom. Stuart Hall, 'New Labour's Double-shuffle', *Review of Education, Pedagogy, and Cultural Studies*, vol. 27, no. 4, 2005; and Stuart Hall, 'New Labour has picked up where Thatcherism left off', *Guardian*, 6 August 2003.

9   Martin Pugh, *Speak for the People!: A New History of the Labour Party*, London: The Bodley Head, 2010, p. 412.

10 Martin Pugh, *Speak for the People!: A New History of the Labour Party*, London: The Bodley Head, 2010, pp. 413–15.

11 Editorial, 'What is at stake?', *Soundings*, no. 2, Spring 1996.

12 Lewis Minkin, *The Blair Supremacy: A Study in the Politics of the Labour Party's Management*, Manchester: Manchester University Press, 2014, Kindle Loc. 372–467.

13 On this backlash, see Dianne Hayter, *Fightback!: Labour's Traditional Right in the 1970s and 1980s*, Manchester: Manchester University Press, 2005.

14 See Frances Stonor Saunders, *Who Paid the Piper?: CIA and the Cultural Cold War*, Granta Books, 1999; and Hugh Wilford, *The CIA, the British*

Left, and the Cold War: Calling the Tune?, Frank Cass Publishers, 2003; Robin Ramsay, *The Rise of New Labour*, Pocket Essentials, 2002; Andy Beckett, 'Friends in high places', *Guardian*, 6 November 2004; Anthony Seldon, *Blair*, The Free Press, 2005, pp. 119–137.

15 The major factor in Labour's defeats continued to be the historic split in its coalition initiated with the defection of the SDP faction in 1981. See Anthony Heath, Roger Jowell and John Curtice, 'Exclusive: How did Labour lose in '92?', *Independent*, 28 May 1994; and Anthony Heath, Roger Jowell and John Curtice, *Labour's Last Chance?: the 1992 election and beyond*, Dartmouth, 1994, p. 285.

16 Lewis Minkin, *The Blair Supremacy: A Study in the Politics of the Labour Party's Management*, Manchester: Manchester University Press, 2014; Liz Davies, *Through the Looking Glass: A Dissenter Inside New Labour*, London: Verso, 2001. Len McCluskey was sufficiently irritated by the Labour leadership's anti-union drive in 2013 to publicly blow the whistle on the Blairites' selections strategy. See Len McCluskey, 'Yes, Labour's selection process has been abused, but not by the unions', *Guardian*, 8 July 2013.

17 Lewis Minkin, *The Blair Supremacy: A Study in the Politics of the Labour Party's Management*, Manchester: Manchester University Press, 2014, Kindle Loc. 2788.

18 Colin Leys, 'The British Labour Party's Transition From Socialism to Capitalism', in David Coates, ed., *Paving the Third Way: The Critique of Parliamentary Socialism*, London: The Merlin Press, 2003.

19 David Coates, *Prolonged Labour: The Slow Birth of New Labour*, Palgrave Macmillan, 2005, pp. 3–23

20 David Coates, '"Darling, It Is Entirely My Fault!" Gordon Brown's Legacy to Alistair and Himself', *British Politics*, no. 3, 2008, pp. 3–21.

21 'Plan to Reduce Budget Deficit', *BBC News*, 2 July 1997.

22 David Coates, *Prolonged Labour: The Slow Birth of New Labour*, Palgrave Macmillan, 2005, pp. 64–5; Simon Rogers, 'UK public spending since 1963', *Guardian*, 26 June 2010; for some background on New Labour policy on spending and employment, see Richard Seymour, *The Meaning of David Cameron*, Zero Books, 2010, pp. 57–8; David Coates, 'A different double shuffle', *Renewal: A Journal of Social Democracy*, vol. 15, no. 2/3, 2007.

23 The first serious exposé of this remarkably corrupt arrangement

between state and privileged sectors of capital was George Monbiot's *Captive State: The Corporate Takeover of Britain*, London: Pan Books, 2001

24   Peter Mandelson and Roger Liddle, *The Blair Revolution: Can New Labour Deliver*, London: Faber & Faber, 1996, p. 48.

25   Gaby Hinsliff, 'Jobless single parents to face benefit cuts', *Observer*, 4 March 2007; Mary Riddell, 'Why Asda Woman matters to Tony Blair', *Observer*, 4 March 2007.

26   Polly Toynbee, 'The Tories were right: workfare really works', *Independent*, 27 February 1997.

27   The analysis of the Institute for Fiscal Studies, not unsympathetic to New Labour, chiefly credits benefit increases and tax credits for falling child and pensioner poverty. Robert Joyce and Luke Sibieta, 'Labour's record on poverty and inequality', Institute for Fiscal Studies, 6 June 2013, ifs.org.

28   Steven Morris, 'Asbo bars suicidal woman from rivers', *Guardian*, 26 February 2005; 'Council withdraws Asbo against boy with Tourette's', Press Association, 28 December 2005; Vikram Dodd, 'Asbo call over jokes about the Pope', *Guardian*, 9 April 2005; Debbie Andalo, 'Teenager handed hoodie ban', *Guardian*, 26 May 2005.

29   'Blair to tackle "menace" children', *BBC News*, 31 August 2006.

30   'Blair "respect" speech in full', *BBC News*, 10 January 2006.

31   See 'Police Service Strength, England and Wales: 31 March 1997 to 30 September 2000', House of Commons Library, Research Paper 01/28, 16 March 2001; and also 'Police workforce, England and Wales: March 2011 supplementary tables', data.gov.uk.

32   In fairness, the prison population had been steadily rising for some time, but the growth very suddenly accelerated from the mid-1990s due to harsher penalties. See 'Story of the prison population 1993–2012', Ministry of Justice, March 2013, gov.uk; and Gavin Berman and Aliyah Dar, 'Prison Population Statistics', House of Commons, 29 July 2013, parliament.uk.

33   'Most prisons are overcrowded – Prison Reform Trust', *BBC News*, 28 August 2012; Jamie Doward, 'Fears that Britain's prisons are at crisis point after growing unrest', *Observer*, 28 March 2015

34   Anushka Asthana, 'New Labour pushed Britain's beliefs to the right, says academic', *Guardian*, 24 January 2010.

35   Patrick Wintour and Vikram Dodd, 'Blair blames spate of murders on black culture', *Guardian*, 12 April 2007.

36   Jack Straw, Interview with Annie Oathen, Radio West Midlands, 22 July 1999; Straw's defecation comments were reported in Vikram Dodd, 'Anger after Straw lets fly at travellers as "crooks"', *Guardian*, 1 September 1999.

37   Rebecca Omonira-Oyekanmi, 'UK immigration detention: the truth is out', *Open Democracy*, 5 March 2015; 'Blunkett names 'Britishness' chief', *BBC News*, 10 September 2002; 'New UK citizenship testing starts', *BBC News*, 1 November 2005; Gaby Hinsliff, 'Speak English at home, Blunkett tells British Asians', *Guardian*, 15 September 2002; Arun Kundnani, *The End of Tolerance: Racism in Twenty-First-Century Britain*, London: Pluto Press, 2007; David Goodhart, 'Too diverse?', *Prospect*, February 2004.

38   The Cantle report, undertaken in response to the northern riots which pitted largely young Asian men against police and the far Right, blamed the 'parallel lives' led by minorities and considered that immigrants should make an oath of national allegiance in future. 'The Cantle Report – Community Cohesion: a report of the Independent Review Team', Home Office, January 2001.

39   'Statistics on Race and the Criminal Justice System – 2004', Home Office, 2005.

40   Charlotte Denny, 'Privately financed revolution', *Guardian*, 3 October 2002; see Allyson Pollock, *NHS Plc: The Privatization of Our Healthcare*, London: Verso Books, 2004; Allyson Pollock, 'The exorbitant cost of PFI is now being cruelly exposed', *Guardian*, 26 January 2006.

41   Roy Hattersley, 'It's no longer my party', *Observer*, 24 June 2001.

42   Even the editorial page of the right-wing London paper the *Evening Standard* gave its backing to 'a full-blooded return to nationalisation'. Editorial, 'The State must step in to save our railways', *Evening Standard*, 12 May 2002.

43   Livingstone failed to block the PPP by legal means, but the sheer fiscal inefficiency of the system led to its eventual collapse, as debt-laden companies ended up selling their stake back to Transport for London. 'Mayor loses bid to block PPP for tube', *Guardian*, 30 July 2001; Alexandra Wynne, 'Why the Tube PPP collapsed', *New Civil Engineer*, 20 May 2010.

44 'US attacks stun TUC', *BBC News*, 11 September 2001.

45 '20,000 join anti-war protest', *Guardian*, 13 October 2001.

46 'Anti-war protests under way', *BBC News*, 31 October 2002.

47 On the *Observer*'s lamentable record of reporting in this period, see Nick Davies, *Flat Earth News: An Award-winning Reporter Exposes Falsehood, Distortion and Propaganda in the Global Media*, London: Vintage, 2009.

48 'Anti-war rally makes its mark', *BBC News*, 19 February 2003; Euan Ferguson, 'One million. And still they came', *Observer*, 16 February 2003.

49 '"Unpopularity is the price of leadership"', *Guardian*, 17 February 2013.

50 'Full text: David Blunkett's speech', *Guardian*, 2 October 2003.

51 Nick Cohen, 'Going nowhere fast', *Observer*, 12 October 2003.

52 Benedict Brogan, Toby Helm and George Jones, 'Union chiefs give Blair bloody nose', *Telegraph*, 2 October 2003.

53 John Kampfner, 'The Warwick watershed', *Guardian*, 2 September 2004.

54 Shiv Malik, 'Occupy London's anger over police "terrorism" document', *Guardian*, 5 December 2011; Daniel Evans, 'Police cracking down on Bristol rioters and extremists', *Bristol Post*, 13 September 2013.

55 John Kampfner, 'Labour's steady path to authoritarianism', *Telegraph*, 19 October 2007; Paul Lewis, 'Birmingham stops Muslim CCTV surveillance scheme', *Guardian*, 17 June 2010.

56 '"Remove full veils" urges Straw', *BBC News*, 6th October 2006; Jonathan Freedland, 'If this onslaught was about Jews, I would be looking for my passport', *Guardian*, 18 October 2006.

57 Andrew Rawnsley, *The End of the Party: The Rise and Fall of New Labour*, London: Penguin Books, 2010, pp. 1397–98; 'In full: Tom Watson's resignation', *BBC News*, 6 September 2006.

58 Toby Helm, 'Disillusioned Jack Straw plotted against Gordon Brown in bid to take over No. 10', *Observer*, 21 February 2010; Decca Aitkenhead, 'Jack Straw: "I would have done a better job than Gordon Brown"', *Guardian*, 31 January 2014.

59 Stephen Nickell, 'The Assessment: The Economic Record of the Labour Government since 1997', *Oxford Review of Economic Policy*, vol. 18, no. 2, 2002; David Coates, *Prolonged Labour: The Slow Birth of New Labour*, Palgrave Macmillan, 2005, pp. 17–184.

60 Gordon Brown, all too late, acknowledged his role in this. Patrick

Wintour and Nicholas Watt, 'Brown: I should have done more to prevent bank crisis', *Guardian*, 17 March 2009.

61   Julie Froud, Michael Moran, Adriana Nilsson, Karel Williams. 'Wasting a crisis? Democracy and markets in Britain after 2007', *Political Quarterly*, vol. 81, no.1, 2010, pp. 25–38

62   Ewald Engelen, Ismail Erturk, Julie Froud, Sukhdev Johal, Adam Leaver, Michael Moran, Adriana Nilsson and Karel Williams, *After the Great Complacence: Financial Crisis and the Politics of Reform*, Oxford: Oxford University Press, 2011.

63   Quoted in Jim Pickard, 'Conservatives: the party of business?', *Financial Times*, 3 February 2016; Tim Ross, 'Michael Gove aims to be the heir to Tony Blair', *Telegraph*, 15 May 2013.

64   Simon Lee and Matt Beech, eds., *The Conservatives Under David Cameron: Built to Last?*, London: Palgrave Macmillan, 2009, pp. 13 and 21–2; especially Stephen Driver, '"Fixing Our Broken Society": David Cameron's Post-Thatcherite Social Policy', in Simon Lee, and Matt Beech, eds., *The Conservatives under David Cameron: Built to Last?*, London: Palgrave Macmillan, 2009.

65   Jon Cruddas and Jonathan Rutherford, 'Labour must fashion a new patriotism', *Guardian*, 1 July 2011.

66   Don Paskini, 'Blue Labour founder: "Labour should involve EDL supporters"', *Liberal Conspiracy*, 21 April 2011.

67   Dan Hodges, 'We should all be in the dock on immigration', *Labour Uncut*, 19 August 2010.

68   'Prime Minister's questions: The Full Story', *BBC News*, 9 June 2010.

69   Hélène Mulholland, 'Labour will make cuts to welfare budget if it wins 2015 election, says Liam Byrne', *Guardian*, 2 October 2012.

70   Richard Seymour, 'Authoritarianism and free-market orthodoxy in Liam Byrne's welfare ideas', *Guardian*, 4 January 2012.

71   Tom Newton Dunn, 'Prime Minister's questions: The Full Story', *Sun*, 22 April 2011.

72   Rowena Mason, 'Emily Thornberry resigns from shadow cabinet over Rochester tweet', *Guardian*, 20 November 2014.

73   'Miliband steps up attack on SNP as any post-election deal ruled out', *The Herald*, 10 April 2015

74   Andrew Grice, 'Ed Miliband lost the election because he ditched New Labour, says Tony Blair', *Independent*, 10 May 2015.

Notes for Pages 178 to 192

Rowenna Mason, 'Beckett report: Labour lost election over economy, immigration and benefits', *Guardian*, 14 January 2016.

76 Oliver Wright, 'Miliband shows he's a control freak too', *Independent*, 17 February 2011; Patrick Wintour, 'Ed Miliband signs up top Obama adviser David Axelrod for UK election', *Guardian*, 17 April 2014; Rowenna Davis, 'Arnie Graf: The man Ed Miliband asked to rebuild Labour', *Guardian*, 21 November 2012.

77 Adam Bienkov, 'Ed Balls wouldn't reverse anything from Osborne's Budget', Politics.co.uk, 19 March 2015.

5. Prospects: Can Corbyn Win?

1 Charles Eliot Norton, 'The Advantages of Defeat', *The Atlantic*, September 1861.

2 William Green, 'Ronnie Campbell calls for honesty over public sector job cuts', *The Journal*, 15 April 2010.

3 Sam Coates, 'Corbyn still first choice for Labour grass roots', *Times*, 24 November 2015.

4 Compounding the unprecedented decline in living standards, the Conservatives' first post-election budget was set to cost thirteen million families an average of £260 a year. Brian Milligan, 'Budget 2015: Squeeze to hit 13m families, says IFS', *BBC News*, 9 July 2015.

5 Perry Anderson, 'Origins of the Present Crisis', in *English Questions*, London: Verso, 1992, p. 42.

6 Tom McTague, 'Jeremy Corbyn makes first move to rein in rebellious Labour MPs', *Independent*, 12 December 2015.

7 On the category of 'social sadism', see China Miéville, 'On Social Sadism', *Salvage #2: Awaiting the Furies*, November 2014.

8 Interview with Phil Burton-Cartledge, 19 February 2016.

9 For an evaluation of how far the term already applies, see Richard Seymour, 'Labour, Pasokified', *Salvage* online, May 2015.

10 John Mann, 'More positions than the Kama Sutra – and not up to the job', *Daily Mail*, 13 September 2015.

11 Jim Pickard, 'Unions refuse to fund Corbyn supporters group', *Financial Times*, 25 February 2016

12 Interview with Liam Young, 13 March 2016; Interview with anonymous Labour activist, 26 February 2016.

13 Freddie Sayers, 'Bernie Sanders, Jeremy Corbyn and their new coalitions on the left', *Guardian*, 15 February 2016.

14 Interview with Margaret Corvid, 25 March 2016

15 Nicholas Watt, 'Labour split exposed as Tom Watson describes Momentum as a "rabble"', *Guardian*, 4 December 2015.

16 Stephen Bush, 'Senior Momentum member expelled from Labour', *New Statesman*, 24 February 2016.

17 Andrew Gilligan, 'Revealed: The radical hard-left Momentum activists mounting a ruthless purge of Labour', *Telegraph*, 13 February 2016.

18 Though, as is always the case, it depends on how you ask the polling question. See Patrick Worrall, 'FactCheck: Does Britain want to scrap Trident?', Channel 4 News Factcheck blog, 4 November 2015.

19 Will Dahlgreen, 'Nationalise energy and rail companies, say public', YouGov, 4 November 2013.

20 The energy companies are, notably, even more unpopular. Tom Clark, 'Energy giants more disliked than banks, poll finds', *Guardian*, 25th January 2015.

21 Will Dahlgreen, 'Voters choose greater equality over greater wealth', YouGov, 30 April 2014.

22 'Corbyn still first choice for Labour grass roots', Office for National Statistics, 22 January 2015, ons.gov.uk.

23 Jeremy Corbyn, 'Building a Social Movement', in Tom Unterrainer, ed., *Corbyn's Campaign*, Nottingham: Spokesman Books, 2016, p. 10.

24 George Eaton, 'How John McDonnell is trying to reframe the economic debate', *New Statesman*, 20 November 2015.

25 Chris Giles, 'Team McDonnell: meet Labour's seven economic advisers', *Financial Times*, 28 September 2015.

26 Gavin Stamp, 'What we learnt about Labour's economic policy from McDonnell's speech', *BBC News*, 28 September 2015; Mariana Mazzucato, *The Entrepreneurial State: Debunking Public vs. Private Myths in Risk and Innovation*, Anthem Press, 2013.

27 See Tony Wood, 'Good Riddance to New Labour', *New Left Review* 62, March–April 2010

28 Andrew Grice, 'It's time that we valued people over profits, poll results show', *Independent*, 24 December 2011.

29 The British Social Attitudes Survey of 2009 found this shift across the board: 'The public now appear less supportive of "big government"

than at any time since the late 1970s'. British Social Attitudes 27 Report, NatCen, December 2010, natcen.ac.uk.

30   James Schneider, 'Jeremy Corbyn can lead the Labour Party back to power', *Prospect*, 12 February 2016.

31   Ipsos Mori, 'Generations', ipsos-mori-generations.com.

32   Andrew Grice, 'Voters "brainwashed by Tory welfare myths", shows new poll', *Independent*, 4 January 2013.

33   Will Dahlgreen and Will Jordan, 'Osborne's first all-Tory Budget: initial scorecard', YouGov, 9 July 2015

34   Raymond Williams, 'Culture Is Ordinary', in Williams, *Resources of Hope: Culture, Democracy, Socialism*, London and New York: Verso, 1989.

35   Glen O'Hara, 'How is Jeremy Corbyn's Labour faring in elections so far?', *New Statesman*, 4 January 2016.

36   Hardeep Matharu, 'Britain could be more left-wing than people assume, study finds', *Independent*, 15 January 2016; Jon Stone, 'Labour seen as "indistinguishable from the Tories" to Scottish voters, leaked internal report warns', *Independent*, 25 January 2016.

37   Ian Johnston, 'Labour was not too left wing for voters at last election, review concludes', *Independent*, 15 January 2016.

38   'Labour opinion poll ratings "worst since World War II"', *Herald*, 19 January 2016.

39   Glen O'Hara, 'How is Jeremy Corbyn's Labour faring in elections so far?', *New Statesman*, 4 January 2016.

40   Interview with anonymous Labour activist, 19 February 2016

41   Interviews with: anonymous Labour activist, 11 February 2016; and Phil Burton-Cartledge, 19 February 2016.